D0700250

Hornblower's *Ships*
their history &
their models

Copyright © 2000 Martin Saville

First published in Great Britain in 2000 by Conway Maritime Press,
a division of Chrysalis Books Ltd, a member of the Chrysalis Group plc,
9 Blenheim Court, Brewery Road, London N7 9NT
www.conwaymaritime.com

A member of the Chrysalis Group plc

British Library Cataloguing in Publication Data
A record for this title is available upon request from the British Library

ISBN 0 85177 783 X

All rights reserved. Unauthorised duplication by
any means contravenes applicable laws.

Martin Saville has asserted his moral right under the Copyright,
Design and Patents Act 1988, to be identified as the Author of this work.

Designed by Wladek Szechter

Printed and bound by Book Print, Spain

Hornblower's *Ships*

their history & their models

Martin Saville

Contents

Acknowledgements

Special thanks to David MacGregor and Andrew Mollo, who gave me the opportunity to be involved in the building of the Hornblower fleet. My warm thanks go to those people who helped in Russia – Sergei, who is a good friend and interpreter, and Pavel, Misma, Alexander, 'Elephant' and all the others in the workshop. At Pinewood, thanks to Martin Gutteridge and Roy Field who, with all the men and women at Effects Associates, brought the models to life for the screen. Finally, thanks to John Lee and Daniel Mersey at Conway Maritime Press, for seeing my project through the editorial process from start to finish.

"Come aboard, sir."
"You name?" asked Masters,
after waiting for a moment.
"H-Horatio Hornblower, sir.
Midshipman," stuttered the boy.
"Very good, Mr. Hornblower," said
Masters, with the equally formal
response. "Did you bring your
dunnage aboard with you?"
Hornblower had never heard that
word before, but he still had enough
of his wits about him to deduce what
it meant.
"My sea chest, sir. It's – it's
forrard, at the entry port."

Mr. Midshipman Hornblower

Two of the 4-metre frigates catching the wind
off the Black Sea during a break in filming.
The sky in the Yalta photographs is a natural one.

Introduction

Several media production companies had looked at the possibility of making films from C.S. Forester's series of books featuring the fictional late eighteenth-century naval hero Horatio Hornblower and his career during the Napoleonic wars, fought between the Royal Navy and the navies of France and Spain. Forester's stories were based on and inspired by actual reports written by officers in the Royal Navy at the time of the wars, which were simplified by Forester to make the characters and their adventures more believable to a book reading public.

The production company which eventually had the commercial prowess, foresight and finances to make the books come to life for the small screen had previously made the successful series about another fictional Napoleonic character, Bernard Cornwell's Sharpe, a soldier whose adventures had been firmly land-based. Horatio Hornblower's adventures differ from Sharpe's in one major aspect – many of his tales are set on board ships at sea. Fifty years ago, a feature film starring Gregory Peck had been successful but had tried to condense Hornblower's life into one feature film (this film was entitled 'Captain Horatio Hornblower', and was made in 1951). The television series that this book refers to commences at the beginning of Hornblower's naval career and looks set to trace it through to the end. Aside from the actors and sets which are an essential part of a film's narrative, this story has another set of players – the ships themselves.

Andrew Mollo was the designer responsible for the commissioning and design of all of the sets for the first two episodes; he organised the manpower, undertook most of the location research, and was responsible for selecting the drawings from which the models would be built. Having been appointed, Andrew soon discovered that he had a problem. Where was he going to find a small fleet of contemporary eighteenth-century ships to play the various roles described in the original books? He looked around the world for any number of suitable survivors and found the most obvious ones quite easily. They included HMS *Victory* at Portsmouth (Nelson's flagship at Trafalgar), *Constitution* (still floating in Boston), and HMS *Trincomalee* (being restored at Hartlepool in England). Although these ships are from the correct period it is not possible to move them and they are too valuable to be rented out to a film company as props and sets. The organisations responsible for the running and maintaining of these ships were very helpful and co-operative, but the conclusion was that as historical references these vessels were fine, but to use them for filming purposes was out of the question. Other ships which were considered include HMS *Endeavour* (a modern replica of Cook's exploration vessel) and the replica of HMS *Bounty* used in a film of the same name. A few others were given consideration but they were all, for various reasons, either unavailable when required or were too expensive. Part of the solution was to build replicas of the ships described by Forester in his books.

A ship called the *Phoenix* was at an early stage of construction in Turkey for another film which had been shelved and the building work had already been finished by the production company in co-operation with the ship's owner Mike Turk. The completed ship would soon become Captain Pellew's HMS *Indefatigable*, the principal ship of Horatio Hornblower's early fictional career. A Baltic trader built in the 1930s was found and modified to play the other full-sized ship used in the production. This left the problem of the remaining ships and ships' boats, which have many different parts to play in the narrative. A small fleet of models, together with full-size replicas (in the case of ships' boats) formed the solution.

The full-sized HMS *Indefatigable* replica – the *Grand Turk* – at her harbour mooring in Artek harbour, Yalta.

HMS *Justinian* being prepared for a close-up shot with the camera to the right, at Pinewood Studios.

The project begins - at work in Russia

To build large models anywhere in the Western world is an expensive exercise, even for the television film world. There are many modelmaking companies in Europe and America who would have made a very good job of building the eleven models required, but the cost would have been prohibitively high and the series would probably never have been made. There are also many boatyards who would have welcomed the opportunity to build the replicas of the ships' boats – especially the two large ones. The production company had made most of the Sharpe films in the Ukraine during the early 1990s and used their contacts in Russia to find a Russian company who would be prepared to build the models at a realistically modest price. A shipyard was eventually found in northern Russia in the city of Petrozavodsk, which when translated means 'Peter's factory'. This derelict shipyard had built five full-size replicas of late eighteenth-century sloops for western buyers in the previous five years and therefore had some understanding of constructing Hornblower's miniature fleet.

My own experience of eighteenth-century navies has been gained from my research for building a significant number of model ships, primarily from the Nelson era, as a hobby for the last twenty-five years. The models which I had built at home were mostly in a loose dockyard style, with as much detail as I could find by reading maritime reference books. Although I am a professional model maker, and am presently working on another film, I feel that the chance of building another fleet like that required for the Hornblower project is extremely remote.

My position on the production team was as consultant model maker which meant that I had no executive power – I could only advise. Much of my time during the construction phase was spent interpreting the various drawings of the models and advising on the easiest way to make the various component parts within the limits of time, processes and materials available locally. If I found that there was a process which was readily obtainable in England, I would purchase the necessary materials or tools and demonstrate to the workforce in Russia how to get the best from them. The main aim was to ensure that everyone's time was used effectively – time was not wasted on anything that the camera did not see. A part of my role (which came as a surprise) was that I had to advise on how a ship from the late eighteenth-century would have looked historically and how this could be applied to the models. Before I departed for Russia I had spent time in Portsmouth photographing what I thought would be the most useful aspects of HMS *Victory*. I spent quite a lot of time exploring contemporary paintings by artists who are acknowledged as faithful recorders of ship's portraits – such as Nicolas Pocock, John Luny and any others who satisfied the criteria. The works of painters such as Turner, although they are great artists, are not reliable as reference sources – he changed proportions and uses a lot of artistic licence, seeing the paintings and its

The fireship set with construction complete is ready for painting. The position of the set allows a view of the sea in the background to give the illusion that it is floating. In the foreground is a small water tank from which Hornblower boards the fireship from a small boat. The large box structure on the deck is the compass binnacle; the mast-like structure is for the ship's rigging to be attached to.

This set presented the production designers with a reference problem because it had to be matched with the fireship models – the drawings of which had long since disappeared into the Russian system never to be seen again. To obtain dimensions for this set, the model was photographed and measured and the production department worked from these calculations to produce the set.

effects as more important than its subject. Scenes on board ships are not so easily found, but there are a good number of contemporary lithographs which often give useful insights and information.

I had been told, before I left for Russia in August 1997, that all the relevant research had been done for the models and sent to the builders. I found this research material much later, too late in fact, in a drawer in the set production office after the models had been built from my own research. One of the major problems throughout the project was that we were building models of the full-sized ships to be used in the production, which either had not been purchased at the time or for which their construction drawings had not yet been completed. This caused many delays and problems, which added to the frustration. Additionally, communica-

A view of the stern of the model of HMS *Indefatigable* at Pinewood Studios.

tions in Russia were erratic to say the least. The production office that produced the drawings which we needed was several thousand miles away in Yalta (in the Crimea). I would try to contact the Yalta office at least once a week to update myself on the current state of affairs and to report on the progress of the models. This exercise frequently took several hours to achieve on the Russian phone system and we were frequently cut off mid call. The net result of this was that many of the models had to be frequently modified to match the full-sized ships of which they were supposed to be small scale copies.

I took a few reference books with me to help me do my job and to read for pleasure in my spare time. These books were continually consulted and I contented myself in the evenings with novels, because the reference books were so popular with the staff who worked in the office. They had never seen reference books of this nature before. The works of Lees and Marquardt were too invaluable, to mention only two examples. A full list of those reference books used can be found in the bibliography. We had an amusing occasion whilst we were using a questionable Russian translation of Karl Heinz Marquardt's book *Eighteenth-Century Rigs and Rigging*, the only translation of any of the books that I had with me, and I was referring to the English version. When my interpreter compared the two we soon realised that the Russian translator had done some serious editing by chopping out whole paragraphs and sentences. Up until this point we had not surprisingly had some serious misunderstandings about details on the sails.

The wealth of detail required to render these model ships convincing to a camera from a number of points of view were, I thought, familiar to me from the building of my own models. However, in many aspects the ship models built for the Hornblower series were completely different. They were designed to be seen

above

Looking up the mast of one of the 4-metre frigates. Note the damaged rail on the aft side of the platform. The models were frequently filmed in a damaged condition, but the damage was usually out of view of the camera.

from a view point low in the water and never closer than 3 metres (9 feet) – the viewpoint of an observer in a rowing boat. This meant that many of the deck details, such as deck planking, were not included since they could not be seen by the camera. Anything which could be seen protruding above the hull's rail was of course made and fitted in its appropriate position. Some of these visible deck fittings included davits, bitts and wheels, cabin doors. Some deck gratings, shot garlands, gun carriages and most of the other deck fittings were not included except on the poop decks (the raised deck at the stern of the ship) which could be seen by our rowing boat observer. The model with most detail on its deck was the 74-gun HMS *Justinian* – Midshipman Hornblower's first ship. All of the models were designed to spend a great deal of time floating on the water. Most of the models were in the water for as long as seven weeks without a break during the filming. This may sound obvious, but most hobbyists' models do not spend much more than a few minutes, if any time at all, in water depending on the purpose for which they were built. The Hornblower models, after a few weeks in the water, were reaching the point where serious consideration was given to applying anti-fouling paint on their bottoms. The size of these models was another consideration. The smallest ones were 4 metres (13 feet) long and the largest was 7 metres (23 feet) long, although this one was eventually not used in the first episodes of the series. The length cited is that of the hull and does not include bowsprits and driver booms (parts of the masts and spars), overhanging the sterns of the model ships.

The original plan was to film the smaller models in a specially constructed tank built for them by the Hornblower production company in Yalta, situated on the peninsular of the Crimea in the former southern Russian state of the Ukraine. The tank is situated in an annexe of Yalta Studios on Polikur hill overlooking the Black Sea, and Yalta Studios is one of the oldest studios in the former Soviet Union dating back to the beginning of the twentieth century.

The larger models had been designed to be filmed in the open sea using a natural background, but this was to prove impossible as the film crew would have had no control over sea or wind conditions. This situation seems to have arisen out of a misunderstanding between the design team and the Ukrainian model director and this in turn contributed to the major problems caused by the fact that the main tank was far too shallow to convincingly accommodate the larger models.

Transportation of the finished models from Petrozavodsk to Yalta was a serious problem; the distances are vast and the road system in Russia is sadly neglected. Local transport companies were used at first but as time progressed Western transport companies were used to transport the models. Various problems were encountered by the production company with the model's tank. The most pressing and frustrating problem was that the tank was built with a water depth too shallow for even the smaller models to float comfortably, let alone be sunk for some of the film sequences. The only remedy was to deepen the tanks and work was duly commenced. Delivery dates on some of the models were delayed and much of the equipment which was to have been supplied by Yalta studios proved to be badly

opposite page, bottom left
Painting the stern of the English frigate in the doorway of our dark Nissen hut in Polikur. In the background to the right is a fireship, and in the far background is the French frigate being prepared for painting.

opposite page, bottom centre
A bow view of one of the 4-metre frigates showing detail of the scumbled paint below the waterline, intended to give the impression of marine growth.

opposite page, bottom right
One of the roles *Grand Turk* played was the French ship *Papillon*. This is a view which could not be seen on the screen, because the *Papillon* colour scheme was only painted on the port side facing away from the camera. Some of the decoration on the transom was also changed for these scenes.

made and in many cases not of much practical use. The equipment also often arrived late after much argument and frustration and when finally received it was found to be old, badly maintained and unreliable. Even brand new, specially-constructed equipment such as the crane built to lift and lower the models into the tank broke down minutes after it had been put to use for the very first time. The first model into the deepened tank had to be lifted in by hand – an undertaking fraught with difficulties because of the model's size and weight (even with the reduced ballast to make it light enough to lift by the many helping hands).

The workshops in which the models were built lay on the shores of Lake Onega, an overnight train away. The workforce had gained their wooden shipbuilding experience constructing the company's main product – wooden sloops of eighteenth-century design. They had a wealth of practical knowledge, but the workshops themselves were crude and out-dated, with the majority of equipment and machinery long past its prime. I gained an enormous respect for these local craftsman who frequently worked in temperatures well below freezing and who produced exceptional results with very basic hand tools. These men were led by a remarkable, well informed and educated man – Pavel Martiukov – who had learnt his shipbuilding skills in the old Soviet-run shipyards of Murmansk. The working practices used by the Russian workforce can be accurately described as antiquated. In a British modelling workshop, the model maker or team, depending on the size and complexity of the model, will be given a verbal briefing and the relevant drawings and materials will be stored readily to hand in the workshop. He/she will have their own hand tools including chisels, saws, measuring equipment and small power tools like jigsaws and cordless drills. The methods and processes employed, unless pre-specified, are left entirely to the modeller's discretion. Problems encountered during the construction and building process are usually resolved by the model-makers themselves; they are given very little in the way of guidance and will draw heavily off of each other's experience. To be fair to the Russian workers, they may have had experience of building full-size wooden ships, but they had not previously built models of any size. In the offices at the yard was a young man – Sasha – whose sole responsibility was to break down the drawings of the models into worksheets which would be given to each worker, or team on a daily basis. These worksheets were usually on a piece of A5 paper, containing beautifully worked scale drawings of the part or part's that the workers were to make that day. All of the dimensions and materials, usually wood, were itemised, complete with a brief description of how the part was to be made and where it fitted into the overall scheme of the model. Any specialised tools needed to produce the part would be itemised so that he could sign for it when collecting it from the workshop tool store. Each man had a personal tool kit which, so far as I could see, consisted of a rudimentary set of tools, most of which were worn out and of ancient design. None of the men had any personal power tools – most of the equipment I saw for sale in local shops was beyond their financial means, because the prices were only slightly cheaper than in the more affluent West. I did see locally made tools in some stores

The complete and painted 74-gun ship HMS *Justinian* in the water at Pinewood. This model had more decoration on its stern than any other ship in the series. Of all the models, this is probably the most historically accurate because it was based upon an actual ship and the colour scheme was taken from several contemporary sources. Before filming, the paint – which was still too new looking to this stage – would be muddied up to give the impression of a ship that has been at sea and weathered.

which were cheaper, but they were very basic. This has to be set against a background of the men's pay; the highest paid skilled worker would earn US$40 a week, whilst the younger apprentices were earning as little as US$20.

I had been alerted to the situation before I left for Russia, and I had purchased many power tools, hand tools and other equipment on behalf of the production company. These included jigsaws, electric planers, modelmakers drills (dremels), sanders of various sizes, and adapters to fit the local plug sockets (plugs and sockets wherever I went seemed to be in short supply). To overcome the supply problem, bare wires were connected to the main power supply with no regard for personal safety. I took Milliput (a two-part modelling putty) by the case load, resin for casting, and silicone rubber for the moulds. When materials which are not readily available locally are taken for use in Russia, you have to think of everything that might be needed – including materials like plasticine to make the moulds up in and spatulas and containers in which to mix the silicone rubber.

Everything happened at a much slower pace than I have been used to, but I did find the northern Russians very open to new ideas if you were patient with them although, as Sergei warned me, the same was not true in the Ukraine.

The production company had originally planned for the four two-hour episodes to be filmed in and around Yalta, and the live action (involving actors) scenes at sea would be filmed seaborne off of the Yalta coast. The models would be filmed at the same time by a Ukrainian film crew in the specially-built tank. I arrived sometime ahead of schedule, so I occupied my time checking that the few

A view of the tank at Pinewood, looking towards the area from where the camera filmed from. The *Julia* model can be seen on the right, and several wind machines line the edge of the tank. The tall metal structure to the right of centre is a dump tank, used to make large waves.

models that had arrived were in good condition, and I started to prepare them for painting. We had a shortage of good interpreters but I got by well enough with the Ukrainian model team by using my pigeon Russian and universal sign language. It soon became apparent that the Ukrainians regarded the model filming very much as their own show, and so I contented myself with painting the models as I had been advised. Weeks passed and it became obvious that our delivery dates had all but been forgotten by our Russian associates. I had left Petrozavodsk earlier than intended because the management of the Hornblower production company changed, and there was some doubt as to whether the production would go ahead at this time. This impasse allowed me an unexpected month at home. Preparations for filming on the tank were slowing down for various reasons, although they had half of the models in place. Unfortunately, all the models were delivered to Yalta too late to be used for the purpose for which they were intended, and something eventually had to give. Several tense weeks later at a meeting between myself, the producers Andrew Benson and Peter Richardson, the director Andrew Greive, the designer Andrew Mollo, together with the Ukrainian model director and director of photography, matters came to a head. This meeting brought an end to the filming of the models in the Ukraine; too many problems were seen as unsurpassable, many attempts at various shots went disastrously wrong, whilst at the same time a significant part of the production budget was being used up. The model filming was to be transferred to the Pinewood film studios just outside London.

Shortly after this meeting I started to prepare the models for their long journey to Pinewood in England. Suffice to say only two films were completed on the live action (live action means with actors) side in the Ukraine, and very few of the model sequences were successfully shot on the specially built tank. None of the special effects shots using the models were successful. The production team had filmed most of the Sharpe series in and around Yalta and were therefore used to the conditions there; Hornblower caught everyone by surprise. Filming at sea is a considerably longer and more tedious business at the best of times, but was exacerbated by the major language and operational differences that were experienced. With only four hours of filming complete out of the eight originally planned, the production company left Yalta in early December 1997 and planned to complete the live scenes for the two missing episodes in Portugal the following year. I proceeded to Pinewood.

As I said, the film crew left Yalta in early December but the models were significantly delayed by bureaucracy and eventually they arrived at Pinewood safely, early in the new year. I had packed the models ready for transportation in a dark 'shed' at Yalta studios. This entailed carefully derigging them, disconnecting all of the rigging and sails and carefully rolling it up. The masts were safely lifted out of their mountings, complete with all of the rigging, and were then carefully laid on the empty decks. The released rigging was now bound to the free masts ready for transportation. All of the loose fittings such as anchors, guns, hatch covers, wheels, spare sails, spars, and binnacles. were either packed into the empty interiors of the hulls or stowed in packing cases. I returned to England to reflect upon my experiences after having been away for almost a year.

Back to England - progress at Pinewood

For several weeks, Pinewood studios had been talked of in the Ukraine as an end to all our trials and tribulations. I had heard so much about how well the job of filming these much travelled models could be done at our new destination. Discussion had, however, taken place about other tanks situated around the world. The 'Titanic' tank in the Mexican desert where the special effects for the blockbuster film of the same name had been made. Malta also had a tank, but I gather that would have created more logistical problems than it would have solved. The original idea of filming the larger models at sea was immediately dismissed because, as it was pointed out to me by wiser heads, they had enough problems filming full-size ships, which are relatively stable platforms, let alone having to rely on a small pontoon bobbing about with a camera fixed to it, and handlers struggling to position a large heavy model for filming. In short, there were too many variables and the film industry always likes to keep things simple. As I learnt at Pinewood, most special effects are designed to be as straightforward as possible to minimise the chances of something going wrong in front of the camera. My primary concern was for the models, ensuring that they had survived undamaged after the long journey across Europe. When I arrived at Effects Associates, the company commissioned to film the models in their large tank at the back of Pinewood studios, I was pleasantly

above

A close up of the bow of *Grand Turk*.
The figurehead is yet to be made and fitted.

top right

The transom of the *Grand Turk* as HMS
Indefatigable. All the carved decorations are
made from solid wood on the full-sized ship.

surprised to find the models all safely on their cradles in a sound stage; they all were intact and had only superficial damage, which was to be expected from such a journey and could be easily repaired. Martin Gutteridge of Effects Associates, the director of the model shoot, had them all unpacked and placed in the dry for assessment and preparation. It could clearly be seen, for the first time, what was needed to prepare them for filming. They all needed rerigging and assembly, and the damage inflicted upon them when filming in the Ukraine and incurred during transit, could now be repaired. On average, it had taken at least a week to rig one of the models in the Ukraine, and I was astounded and relieved that, without the language barrier, this task took half the time in England. Moving the models was easy and fork lift trucks made light work of moving them; there was no more struggling with levers and collapsing casters on the model's cradles. The masts and spars had all been mixed up in transit, but with all of the models in a well lit warm environment this problem was soon solved. Martin Gutteridge had assembled a very competent team of film technicians who, with the relaxed air of people who had seen it all before, made the time at Pinewood a very positive experience. Within a month, the first models were ready for their debut in front of the camera. Most of them were repaired, rigged, painted and modified for the various scenes in which they were to act. The unfinished ones were completed while the film progressed. There were many problems but they no longer caused the delays they had in Yalta; the technicians would always have something which reduced the problem to easily manageable proportions. If we needed something which was unavailable in the studio complex, which was rare, we could jump into a car and go to purchase it there and then. Different sizes of rope were needed to repair the models rigging, and during a phone call to ascertain if what we wanted was available from a rope warehouse, we were spoilt for choice. No longer were we robbing one model to repair the damage on another, and consequently we were saving time. We now even had scaffold towers which also gave access to the masts and sails.

Additional sets and craft

Aside from the fleet of models now assembled at Pinewood there were a number of additional craft, which though not in the strictest terms models, were nevertheless essential to the filming of the production. While I was in Petrozavodsk, two full-size ships' boats were built – a twenty-oared long-boat 12 metres (39 feet) in length and a fourteen-oared cutter 10 metres (33 feet) long. Two smaller boats were also used which had been built for another customer before I arrived; these were purchased by the production company. In Sevastopol a large pontoon was converted into a floating set. It was based on a section of a full-sized 74-gun ship complete with deck fittings and lower decks, a full scale section of gun deck and reconstructions of the accommodation which would have been part of an eighteenth-century ship of the line. This craft will be described in more detail later since it was to play a major part in the first two Hornblower episodes and one of the models was built to match this set. For the fireship sequence, a full-sized set was built for Dennis Lawson and Ioan Gruffudd to perform their heroic deed of saving HMS *Indefatigable*. There were of course many other sets which are beyond the brief of this book and I had very little involvement in them.

The 20-oared, 12-metre longboat in Artek harbour, Yalta, painted and varnished in one of its many colour schemes. In the background is the *Grand Turk* (HMS *Indefatigable*) tied up at her berth. The harbour was the main base for the *Julia*, *Grand Turk* and all of the other seaborne operations for the Hornblower production company in the Ukraine.

The background to Hornblower

A very brief sketch of the historical background to the Napoleonic Wars (1793-1815), in which the Hornblower stories are set, is helpful to put the series in context. Britain had been at war with France and Spain intermittently for over one hundred years before the fictional hero Hornblower appeared on the scene to start his career. At the end of the eighteenth-century, and although often described as conservative in its approach to new ideas, the British Navy had made great progress in the development and design of warships and their construction methods through such men as the naval architect Sir Robert Seppings (1767-1840). A great period of exploration was occurring during the period with people such as James Cook (1728-79) charting previously unaccounted for lands in the interests of trade. For Britain to have safe passage for its trading ships, it needed to have a navy which could defend those sea lanes aggressively. To this end it developed the most powerful navy of its day. Hornblower's fictional career was to last long enough to see the end of the major seaborne conflict between the allied French and Spanish navies and the British navy culminating in the Battle of Trafalgar on 21 October 1805. However, the war was to continue until the Battle of Waterloo on 18 June 1815.

The creator of Horatio Hornblower, C.S. Forester (1899-1965), started his career as a writer of fiction after having failed the anatomy examinations of his chosen career in the medical profession. As a promising young English writer he was invited to Hollywood in the 1930s to work as a script writer on the booming movie business. It was on Forester's voyage back to England that the character of Hornblower was formulated, primarily as the heroic character of a single novel. This first novel, Mr Midshipman Hornblower, set the foundation for the entire Hornblower series, comprising ten novels which have remained enduringly popular across the world to the present day. Forester had the skill of continuing an expressive and highly convincing narrative style with an acute historical understanding of the Napoleonic wars and life aboard ship. He used the *Naval Chronicle*, a monthly magazine published between 1790 and 1820, to great effect and took from it numerous details of naval actions, equipment and seamanship and incorporated those into his narrative.

The character played by Robert Lindsay in the television series, Captain Pellew, was based on a real person. Like all officers of his day Admiral Edward Pellew (1757-1833) had entered the Royal Navy as a midshipman, in 1770. His career was prolific and promotion swift as he progressed through the Revolutionary War (1793-1801). He became an Admiral in 1804 when despatched to the East Indies as Commander-in-chief. Pellew's most celebrated action, and the one that no doubt brought him to Forester's attention, was the destruction of the 74-gun French ship-of-the-line *Droits de l'Homme* as she returned from Bantry Bay in February 1796. Pellew captained the English frigate HMS *Indefatigable* in the battle, which continued throughout the night in heavy weather just off the French coast. Pellew's career continued until 1821. He had previously been made a viscount, taking the title Lord Exmouth in 1817, following his successful bombardment of Algiers the year before.

opposite

The two *Grand Turk* models have just been craned off the lorry. The shine on the model to the right is caused by sunlight reflecting off of the resin matt which extends up to the model's channels. Some appreciation of the model's size can be gained from the men working on them.

1. Construction

The cable growled a protest as the anchor took it through the hawsehole – that welcome splash of the anchor, telling of the journey's end. Hornblower watched carefully while Le Reve took up her cable, and then relaxed a little. He had brought the prize safely in.

The Duchess and the Devil

Building the models to be used in Hornblower production required two unique sets of skills. The first skills which were needed were those of the eighteenth-century shipwright, to design and construct replica fighting ships of their time; the second were those of the modeller, needed to reproduce accurate details in small scale. That both sets of skills were required was a product of the Hornblower models' size – they were too small to exclusively use the skills of a shipwright, whilst at the same time being too large to use only modellers' techniques. There was no set way around this; we simply had to decide what would look right, considering the size of the model and the camera views which it would be seen at, and choose the right techniques from this starting point.

The hulls

The hulls of the eleven models were constructed in two different ways. Any variations will be highlighted, and a fuller description given when I discuss each individual model. Originally there were to be twelve models, but the French privateer *Le Pique*, which was to have been 6 metres (20 feet) in length and based around the full-sized ship *Julia*, was cancelled before its construction began.

All of the drawings for the models were supplied to the Russian construction team by the designer Andrew Mollo with the exception of the three 4-metre (12 feet) frigates. When Pavel Martuikov, the Russian leader of the construction team, received the model drawings they were in the standard scale for most eighteenth-century ship's drafts, which is a quarter inch on the drawing representing one foot on the full-sized ship, or a scale of 1:48. The models were not built to a particular scale, their hull length was specified on the order given to the builders and the drawings supplied were redrawn by Pavel Martuikov and his drawing assistant Sasha, to meet the hull length specified. Pavel took the drawings and then redrew them taking into account the specifications which he had been given

Inside the workshops in Petrozavodsk, where the models were constructed. On the upper left is the full-sized, carvel-built 20-oared ship's longboat, being planked with pine. The longboat is twelve metres long – the three 4-metre frigates are being fitted out to the right.

(e.g. the hull length and the propeller shaft). The models were approximately one-fifth and one-sixth actual size. He simplified the construction method used in full-sized ship building practice to facilitate a faster building method and to use more modern building materials. This approach was intended to have the effect of delivering the models within budget and on time for the tight film shooting schedule. The specification included waterproof hatches in the deck to give access to the interior of the hulls to enable the crew to load and distribute the ballast. The hatches afforded access to the car batteries which were proposed for use for interior lighting in the cabins. The hatches on the larger models also gave access to the firing guns on the lower deck which would need reloading several times during filming.

The main construction material used in the making of the models was a pine, common to the north of Russia (which is of a reasonable quality because the trees in the local area grow more slowly than some of the readily available varieties grown for the mass markets in the West). Pine was used for all of the main structures, masts and the planking. Birch, which is a fine-grained whiter timber, was used for the finer detail work such as the mouldings on the hull and head rails at the bow. I found this timber had excellent model making properties and was somewhat surprised to find that the Russians regarded it as only suitable for firewood. Birch-faced ply was extensively used for decks, bulkheads, hull lamination and any instance else where sheet material would have been the suitable material of choice. Birch-faced ply is available in Britain and a great deal is exported from the area where the models were built; the locally available plywood is mostly second quality and does not have all of the knots nicely routed out and carefully filled with slivers of birch. PVA wood glues, as far as I could work out, were not easily obtained locally but they were used on the smaller parts. The models were mostly glued together using a locally made two part resin adhesive which seems to work as required. Cyanacrylate or Superglue was supplied to the builders in vast quantities, but for reasons I could not fathom, there was a reluctance to use it very often.

The method used to construct the framing of the models is a much simplified version of full-sized ship building process. Where as a full-sized ship of the eighteenth century was expected to have many years of service in all weathers these models were to be used in a controlled environment. This meant that many short cuts could be made in their construction when compared with their full-sized sisters.

Each model started life on the floor of the rigging room in the offices of Askold, the Russian company hired to build the models. I do not propose to describe in detail how all of the shapes of the profiles were arrived at but I shall give a simplified description. Any ship's hull is a complex shape made up of rib-like frames, attached to the keel (the ship's backbone). The planking is fixed to the outside of these frames, which makes the hull watertight. To obtain the shapes of the frames, the ribs were plotted, to full model size, onto a half breadth plan on a sheet of hardboard. The builder started this process by putting a vertical centre-line down the middle of the board which represented the centre of the keel; this was then marked in and then the widest part of the hull (usually somewhere near the centre

The 74-gun ship HMS *Justinian* in frame.
The built up frames can clearly be seen in this
view. In the background on the left is one of
the three fireships waiting to be fitted out.

of the ship looking from the side) was plotted with an allowance given for the thickness of the planking. The planking on these models varied between 10mm (0.39 inch) on the smaller models and 15mm (0.59 inch) on the larger ones. The hulls were not constructed using as many frames as a full-sized ship, which on a sailing warship could have been as little as one foot apart. They each had fourteen to twenty frames fitted along the keel depending on the finished length with the larger models having more frames than the smaller ones. On a full-sized eighteenth-century warship the frames could be placed so closely together for strength that without the exterior planking on them, they looked almost solid. Anyone who is familiar with building model ships will recognise that you do not require that many frames to obtain the external shape of a ship's hull; the same principle applied here. When the centre frame had been plotted full-size onto the drafting board, the other frames were added with each one becoming smaller as it approached the bow or stern, producing the hull's distinctive shape. Unlike the centre frame all of the others were only plotted in halves, the ones running from the centre to the bow on the right and the others to the stern on the left which is the normal ship building convention. This is done because the frames running along a ship's hull are mirror images of each other. In full-sized practice, looking down from the top of a mast, as the frames approach the bow of the ship they are set at an angle facing forward to the keel, unlike the others which are at ninety degrees to it. These radiate like a fan from the bow end of the keel and are called cant frames allowing the planking a 'fair' run and reducing the possibilities of distortion caused by the planks pulling the frames out of true alignment. If the frames continued at ninety degrees to the keel then the amount of timber, which would have to be removed, to bevel the frame edge and give a flat surface to fix the planks to would have severely weakened the structure of the hull at its most vulnerable point. In these models this method was unnecessary because the planks were sufficiently supported by the closeness of the frames on the keel.

When the body section drawing was completed on the moulding loft board, showing all of the individual frames in half profiles, the next stage of the marking out was added. At about the level of the 'wale' (the broader and thicker strakes of planking around the hull at approximately the level of the lower decks and usually the widest part of the hull) a line was put in which represented the level of the model's gun deck. The shapes of the frames below this line were then traced off to be transferred to the full-sized frame on a template made of a thin sheet of hardboard. These templates did not include any of the shapes of the upperworks, like the poopdeck or the forecastle. The templates only gave the shape of half of the full frame since they are identical on both sides of, and at any given point of, the keel. The frame itself was made up of a series of straight pieces of wood, approximately 150mm (6 inches) by 25mm (1 inch) thick, joined together by lap joints which roughly gave the profile shape of the frame. Screws were put through the joint for added strength. When the two halves of the frame had been assembled, the template was overlaid and the finished profile was drawn onto the frame using the plywood template taken from the moulding loft board drawing. It was then a simple matter to cut the frame's shape out using a band saw or, in the case of the smaller ones, a hand held jigsaw. Each frame at this stage looked like a two dimensional 'U' and across its open end a timber was fixed holding its open ends apart and giving it rigidity. This cross timber would later be the foundation for the construction of the plywood deck. The process was repeated for all the frames.

The keel, to which the frames are attached, was then marked out on one long piece of timber equal in length to that of the model's overall hull. The positions of the frames were marked out and mortices and slots were cut into the keel to accept the frames. The keel was made from two long timbers fixed together to form a 'T' shape in section. At the bow end of the keel the distinctive curved form was made up with as many as ten pieces of timber, all joined together to obtain the curved beakhead shape, which would later be the foundation for the headrails. The stern post, from which the rudder is suspended was made in a similar fashion. The stern post was tenoned into the keel and 'knees' were fitted between the keel and the stern post for support.

The normal practice in full-sized shipbuilding is to make the keel out of several pieces of wood secured by a very strong joint known as a 'scarf'; this is as trees do not normally grow tall enough to make it out of a single piece. Working at

An interior view of the clinker-built, 14-oared cutter. The boat is 10 metres long.

This stern shows the changes to the model after the full-sized ship was changed because the initial choice was found to be 'hogged'. On the deck, one of the hatches can be seen open. This hatch would later be used to load the sandbagged ballast to keep the model upright in the water.

the smaller scale ensured that we did not have such problems and the keels were made of one piece of timber. When the keel was complete the frames were fixed to it to ensure that they were at ninety degrees in two planes – both vertically and horizontally. If they were not positioned squarely to the keel, all sorts of problems would arise. An out-of-square frame leaves a hollow area in the planking thus spoiling its smooth, run and the hull will always look as though it has a dent in it. When all of the frames and the keel had been put together a long timber was screwed and glued on top of the frames just above the keel. This timber roughly approximates to a keelson and had the effect of locking the frames into the keel. The positions of the centres for the three masts, or two in the case of the Julia were now determined and planks were laid running from the two closest frames over the keel to provide a step for the mast to securely socket into. Not all of the models were made in this way and some had their masts stepped directly onto the deck

We now had a long piece of wood with frames sticking out of it like ribs attached to a backbone. To prevent these carefully mounted frames from being knocked out of position a knotch had previously been cut into the outer corner of each frame and a long stringer, or batten, was fixed and ran from the bow to the sternframe. The frames were then faired up, which means a test plank was laid in the same way as the planking would run over the frames to ascertain where the high spots were. These were then sanded or planed down. The frames at the bow and stern had their outside edges bevelled to form a flat surface for the planking to be fixed to.

In the case of the smaller models, all the above construction was completed with the model standing the right way up; the hulls of larger models were made upside down for ease of working. The hulls were now rigid structures ready to have the planking fixed onto them, or to be laminated with plywood. A groove called a 'rabbet' is normally cut into the length of the keel construction which acts as a joint for the first (garboard) plank. This additionally acts to stiffen the keel. In this case the rabbet was dispensed with, except at the bow and stern post, since this was where the planks were going to end; consequently they needed a secure fixing as they would come under severe strain when the planks were bent around the frames.

The planking on a ship usually tapers along the length of the hull to compensate for the rise at the bow and stern. This arrangement of planking on a completed ship gives the illusion that, when viewed from the side, the planks are all the same width.

The Spanish frigate early in its fitting out in the Petrozavodsk workshops, with the gun ports being cleaned up.

Tapering the planks also means that they follow the curve running along the length of the ship, known as the sheer. Timber also does not come in lengths sufficiently long enough to run the entire length of the hull. To counter this they are butted end-to-end in short lengths and fixed with 'tree nails' onto a frame. Tree nails were pieces of well seasoned dry oak. Sometimes circular, sometimes sixteen sided in section, were driven into holes that had been previously bored by an auger, to hold pieces of timber together.

Not all of the planks used to cover the frames were tapered lengths – on many warships they had 'anchor stock' planking as explained here by Longridge (1955):

> This method of planking entailed an expensive consumption of timber, but was considered to afford considerable strength. Each plank was fashioned with a double taper from the centre of one edge, so that two planks laid side by side looked something like the stock of an anchor. The planks were laid so that the middle or broadest part of the plank was immediately above or below the narrow butts of two others. The top and bottom edges of two strakes of planking are parallel.

There were other methods of planking various parts of ships, but the most familiar to modelmakers is the 'stealers', which are used at the stern to make up wide or narrow spaces in the planking run and to keep the planking running in 'fair' lines

The models for the Hornblower series were built to a price which meant that they were planked in the quickest and most economical way to reduce both the amount of timber wasted in tapering planks and construction time. All of the methods which we used were used in the past for very good reasons, primarily to create very strong hulls. However, these methods were time-consuming and were not available to the Hornblower construction team. The construction method used on the models, that of strip planking, whilst not aesthetically pleasing close up, gave the necessary effect once a layer of paint had been applied. From a distance it would be difficult to notice how the planks were running along the ship's side.

To plank the hull, pine was cut into strips 25mm to 58mm (1 inch to 2 inches) wide and approximately 12mm (0.5 inch) thick. Each plank was cut to length and glued and screwed into position with a generous measure of two part resin glue applied to the edges between the planks to give a waterproof joint. Planks were laid edge to edge across the hull on both sides of the keel until they reached the top of the frames. This method, whilst being very quick – a 5 metre (15 foot) hull could be planked in a couple of days – meant that because there were no tapers on the planks at a point around the centre of the hull, the planks started to get shorter towards their middle and very curved along their length. Some shaping of the last planks to be installed was required together with some adjustment and fiddling around the stem and stern. This was, however, very easy in comparison with full-sized practice.

At the bow and stern of each model the planks had to be bent around seemingly impossibly complex curves. In order to bend wood without it splitting or snapping it has to be heated and saturated with hot steam in a steam box – a crude looking long box discharging steam coming out of its ends. All shipyards dedicated to wooden ship construction would have had at least one of these pieces of equipment. The principle is quite simple: a heat source, which in the case of the models was a wood burning stove, boiled water in a sealed boiler with a flexible pipe to feed the hot steam to the enclosed box which was filled with planks that had been cut to the required length. The planks were exposed to the steam for about half an hour, after which time they were flexible, and when one was deemed ready (by simply pulling it and testing it), it was rapidly withdrawn from the box and bent into shape over the frames. Each plank would still be steaming hot when it was placed in its final position since it would simply break if allowed to cool. It would then be glued and screwed into place. After it has been steamed in this way, wood is extremely flexible (for example, I have experimentally tied thin strips of wood into knots using this process). Sometimes however, there would be a loud crackling sound as a hot piece of wood protested at this treatment and broke under the strain. The whole process would then have to be repeated with a new piece of timber until the hull planking was complete. It does sound complicated but when new wood was fed regularly into the box a rhythm of movement amongst the workers could be seen – planks being fixed to the frames and fresh ones being fed into the steam box. I could almost imagine those old shipwrights of the past officiating over their steam boxes at Chatham or Portsmouth dockyards.

The eighteenth-century ship builder would probably start the planking at

The French frigate being prepared for painting in the workshops at Polikur, Yalta. The carved figure on the stern are formed from Milliput. A great deal of the model's preparation and painting was done in a very dark Nissen hut where there was very limited access to any electricity supply.

the keel with comparatively thicker timbers which would get progressively thinner as they went up the side of the hull. However, each individual model had planks which were the same thickness all over the hull. Full-sized practice dictates that as each strake of planks were fixed into position a small gap was left between them along its length. This was so the caulker, using a special long headed mallet and chisel-shaped tool, could hammer lengths of oakum, which is old rope unravelled, tightly into the gap. I pity the prisoners of the past who were given lengths of old rope to unravel for this purpose. After the oakum was inserted, hot tar would have been poured on top to keep it dry. This tedious, tiring and repetitive task was made necessary by the fact that wood expands when wet. The caulker, in effect, filled the gaps left between the planking to compensate for this expansion. The Hornblower models did not need to be caulked however, as we used a generous amount of resin glue, which provided suitable waterproofing; the model's planks were not wide enough to expand and contract so much as to require any further waterproofing.

Upon completion of the planking process, our models were now lying on the floor looking a bit rough and ready, and had little resemblance to eighteenth-century warships. They looked for all the world like someone's idea of a rowing boat without their forecastle or their poop, hard resin everywhere and the edges of planks protruding slightly above the surface and not at all smooth in appearance. The considerable task of sanding had now to be performed. The entire hull had to be sand-

A stern view of the Spanish frigate. Just forward of the rudder can be seen the two anchorage points used for mooring and manoeuvring the models during filming. The upper one was the result of much discussion with the model builders, because we wanted a simple hole drilled through the keel lined with a metal tube for a rope to be passed through. They said the hull was not strong enough and screwed on the plate and loop arrangement which can be seen in this photograph. At Pinewood, these were considered to be too weak and they installed the heavy steel bracket hanging below the keel. These were far more effective, because they were on the centre-line of the model, and the rope's pull did not send the model off course.

ed down smooth with a large electric sanding disc and belt sander. Dust went everywhere and the workers went white with it. When this arduous task had been completed the now smooth surface was carefully dusted off and the area around the model swept clean. The hull's exterior surface was then carefully cleaned using a pungent chemical based on acetone. This chemically cleaned the surface in preparation for the next process – the sealing of the underwater part of the hull. This was done by applying a two part resin onto which, while it was still in an uncured liquid state, a fine fibreglass cloth was carefully stretched over the whole surface in wide overlapping strips, running from one edge over the keel to the opposite edge, until the whole hull had been covered from end to end. Additional resin was then applied to ensure that the surface was smooth and clean looking.

Some of the model's frames were covered in a completely different way to the planking method, by a process called cold moulding which is both quicker and cheaper. However, my concern with this process was that the sides of the models would not have that characteristic planked look. Thin ply is cut into strips approximately six inches wide and the strips are then fitted diagonally down the sides of the frames, abutted to each other and screwed and glued into position. This method is used on many small sailing dinghies, and I believe that it was also used on motor torpedo boats and motor gunboats during the Second World War. My concerns were unfounded though, since the process was only used on areas of the hulls which would be underwater and was never seen on screen. When the process was complete, they had a skin of resin and fibreglass cloth applied to them, just like the planked models.

I mentioned earlier that the lower part of the keel had been omitted. This was added once the resin had hardened overnight when the keel was screwed into its final position and resined. At this stage the beakhead timbers were also screwed into position. I must admit that I was puzzled at first as to why this method was adopted, but I later realised that doing it this way meant that the hull was a sealed unit and it reduced the amount of joints which would allow the ingress of water into the main body of the hull. This method proved to give the models watertight integrity.

6mm (0.2 inch) thick birch plywood was now screwed onto the cross pieces of the frames to form the gun deck. Most of the models had at least two openings in the deck, for access to the inner part of the hull (usually just forward of and just behind the main mast). The 6mm plywood decks later proved to be too thin and started to warp and bend with the many feet walking about on it. The hatch lips were raised about 50mm (2 inches) above the level of the deck so that when water was on the deck it did not flow straight into the hull. There was also a camber across the deck so that water found its way out through the side of the ship via the scuppers down the outside of the hull. The scuppers were simulated by drilling 15mm (0.6 inch) holes into the side of the hull at the upper deck level.

The shape of the upper subframes for the poop and forecastle decks were now taken from the draft plans and the shapes were cut from pine planks and screwed and glued to the plywood deck. Along the top of the frames a stringer was fitted which strengthened the whole assembly. After the completion of frame work for those two decks it was planked over in the same way as the hull. On the bow of most of the models, a beakhead bulkhead was constructed with a small deck where the bowsprit and toilets (heads) are situated. This was made of plywood shaped and fitted to the upper edge of the forward frames and sanded fair. At last the model now had its distinctive shape but lacked any of the fittings.

Now came the process which any modelmaker or shipwright will agree is the most time-consuming – the fitting out. This was not done in any particular order, but one of the first things to be added was the wale, a thicker strip of planking running along the length of a ship at its widest point just above the waterline. This line of planking is easily identified from contemporary paintings because it is usually painted black, in stark contrast to the rest of the hull. The wale had several purposes. It protected the ship's hull when it was up against a harbour wall and like-

above

**A close up of the stern lantern on
the** *Grand Turk*.

above right

The stern of HMS *Justinian*, **doubling as a
Spanish ship. The lanterns have suffered acci-
dental damage, which was a common problem
during filming.**

wise when it was in close action with another ship. It also offered some protection
for the gunners against the enemies ordnance, as they worked at the gun ports just
above it. Large warships with two or more decks also had wales positioned below
the upper gunports.

   We left the hulls as undressed but sanded ship-shaped objects. Starting at
the stern, the first features which greet the eye are the lanterns. Most ships had two,
although the larger first rates had three with another on the back of the mainmast
top. They were used for signalling and for station keeping by ships following at
night. Octagonal in section and cone shaped lengthways, the lanterns are made up
of glazed panels with a small vent at the top to allow the fumes and heat from the
lamp to escape. The inboard face has a door to provide access to the lamp and maintain it. The lanterns on all of the models were designed to work with a small 12-
volt halogen car headlight bulb. The main glazed body structure of the lantern was
made from 3mm (0.1 inch) perspex cut into tapered segments to form the octagonal shape. The roof, vents and the base were made to fit closely into the perspex
body. The bottom is permanently fixed but the upper part is designed to be removable to give access for bulb changing. An orange light filter is used to soften the
harsh halogen light and give the lantern the appearance of an oil lamp. The panels
of the glazed portion were simulated by sticking thin strips of wood on to them. In
full-size practice, most of the lanterns were mounted on the stern with a heavy
metal tripod frame. The model lanterns were mounted on a single curved tube,
which had the wires which gave power to the bulb passed through from the interi-
or of the hull. These lanterns were very prone to damage because of their exposed
position and had to be remade and repaired many times during filming.

   The stern was usually the most decorated area of the fighting ships of this
period. Across its broad curved expanse there were a series of glazed windows; on a

first rate ship, the biggest type of ship from this period, there could be three tiers of these windows. Behind these windows on a large warship was the captain's, officers' and admiral's quarters. On the smaller frigates such as HMS *Indefatigable* this was the private preserve of the captain. The officers' accommodation was in the wardroom somewhere below the captain's quarters. The largest of the ships which were used in the first series of Hornblower was HMS *Justinian*, which had two tiers of windows. All of the others except the *Julia*, which had none, had a single row of windows. Most of the Hornblower models were based upon

A stern view of the Spanish 4-metre frigate after being repaired at Pinewood. The original stern was far more ornate featuring carved mythological figures. The original stern was destroyed during filming in Yalta.

frigates, and during this period there was a reduction in the amount of decoration to be found on warships, because the government was alarmed by the large amounts of money which had been used to decorate them. This is not to say there was no decoration, and a significant amount had to be prepared and mounted onto the models. Most of the decorative features were around the windows and included mythological figures and creatures running up their sides and across the top. Various national emblems, coats of arms and flags were also included. Balustrading, or variations upon that theme, together with mouldings were also a common feature.

All of the decorative features on the models were carved by a Russian art

A view of the stern of the French 4-metre frigate in the tank at Pinewood. The decorative figures were carved from Styrofoam and the finer details were applied with Milliput. The windows are made to give the impression of being sash windows. The sad looking, broken lantern was a common problem during filming because they were very exposed. The model handlers and technicians who had to manoeuvre the heavy models into position for filming were very careful, but inevitably accidents did happen when people are under pressure.

The full-size *Julia* at her moorings in Artek harbour. This photograph was taken as a reference shot for the conversion of the model which was to play the *Marie Galante*. All of the decoration on the stern is easily removable so that the ship can be converted for a different role.

student employed specifically to carry out the work. The main shapes were carved from Styrofoam (a light man-made material which is very easy to cut, abrade and carve with sharp tools). Any final detailing was finished off with carving chisels and riffler files. The finished details were then glued into position on the stern. It was originally intended to ensure that the decorated sterns were easily removable on the small 4-metre frigates, to facilitate the models' change of identity for different scenes – effectively increasing the number of models available for filming. Translation, particularly with regards to building instructions was a problem and the removable stern concept proved less effective than envisaged.

Below this decoration was the counter, which would, in the Nelson era, have had the ships name painted on it. On some of the earlier, larger warships fantastic painted friezes were often to be found here. Below the counter was the rudder hanging from its pintles and gudgeons, which allow it to be turned on the stern post. All the rudders were made from pine cut to the same thickness as the keel. Most rudders were tapered along their length and in section, the wider part towards the stern post. The tiller was usually mounted in a mortice on the upper end of the rudder, inside the hull, but none of the models required tillers or any of the additional equipment associated with steering a ship. They were left to hang, which made them very easy to lift off and stow. The metalwork for the pintless was fabricated and welded by an outside contractor.

Moving forward along the hull, we come to another decorated and glazed area which followed the line forward from the stern. These are quarter galleries, which were small cabins off of the main stern cabin. Their main function was as the officer's toilets, because they overhung the sea and gave a clean run for the waste. They were also used for storage purposes.

Running along the sides of the hull were various strakes and mouldings and these were all glued and screwed into position. The gun ports were cut through the planking and a door was made to be a very easy fit. The hinges were made from strips of aluminium bent over at the end to form a tube. Through this a stiff wire was passed and bent into a 'U'-shape to form the part of the hinge which was hammered into the hull. The hinges were very crude to look at close up, but they performed their task without any trouble.

A close-up of the channels on one of the 4-metre frigates, giving an idea of how the dead eyes and shrouds are secured with a quick release mechanism.

The lower part of the standing rigging on each mast was tensioned by a pair of deadeyes set up on the channels which stuck out from the side of the hull. Beneath the channels are chains linking the deadeyes to the hull and the tension from the standing rigging is usually spread by chain plates bolted through the hull. The chains and plates are made from thick metal wire and steel rods formed into the chain's shape and then welded together to form loose chain links. The shrouds for the lower masts were made to be detachable so that the masts could be lifted out of the mountings complete with their standing rigging. The lower deadeyes had an open ended strop around them on the lower end with a hole for a stiff wire to pass through. This long wire, when pushed through the holes, also passed through the upper end of the chains securing the shrouds to the channel. All of the models had a similar system which worked extremely well.

A stern and bow view of the model of HMS *Indefatigable* at Pinewood Studios.

Down the sides of the hull were various slot shaped holes which normally had a pulley wheel for the sail braces to pass through to be belayed on belaying pin rails; the models had holes drilled through the hull for this purpose. Any other belaying points on the exterior of the hulls were made with simple cup hooks screwed into the appropriate position.

At the bow of most of the models was a basket shaped area called the head timbers. These were a complex array of tapering, curved timbers all coming together at the figurehead. On the upper timbers there was usually a grating which had two to four 'seats of ease' for the convenience of the crew. None of these toilets were fitted to the models.

The boomkins, which act as spreaders for the bowsprit's sail, stick out at a slightly downward angle from the top of the head rails like two cat whiskers. The figureheads, as with the stern decoration, were carved from Styrofoam and in all cases finer detail applied with Milliput modelling putty. All of the figureheads were made to be easily removable, so that when a particular model changed its role for the film, the figureheads were interchangeable. The hawse pipes which normally took the heavy anchor cable into the main body of the hull were drilled holes with the cable hanging loose inside the hull.

Any other visible external fittings were made from wood and usually glued and screwed into their position. When the hulls were complete with all their fittings (with the exception of the masts and the rigging), the interiors were painted with a red oxide primer and the external hull was given a coat of local waterproofing mixture, which proved to be a nuisance because it always remained sticky even after many months. After a lot of scouting around the city, we managed to find a Swedish yacht varnish with which all the other models were treated.

The masts

Before I describe how the masts and yards of the models were constructed, it is necessary to give a brief outline description of the component parts which make them up. Starting at the bow of a ship, there is the bowsprit which points forward at a shallow upward angle. Working aft from the bow, the next mast is the foremast and is generally the second tallest. The mast was usually worked by the more experienced and older seaman because among their other duties was the responsibility for the safe handling of the ship's anchors and manning of the guns on the forecastle (generally the space or decks between the bow and foremast). On some bomb vessels the foremast was used as the tallest, but they usually only had two masts anyway. This would be the mast which the most experienced lookout would be sent up to survey the horizon and hopefully sight enemy ships before being spotted themselves. The mast at the back of the ship is the mizzen and it is the shortest one. This mast was often used as a 'training area' for the young seaman and midshipman because it was under the direct eye of the officers who spent the majority of their time in this area of the ship.

A mast of this period generally consisted of three sections. Starting at the bottom and going upwards, the lower mast, which extended right down below decks to the keelson. The 'topmast' was the middle section and the topgallant was

The fitting out of the 4-metre English frigate is complete and the rigging is progressing. The cold moulding of the underwater areas of the hull can be detected below the resin matting and the styrene figurehead is waiting to be filled and painted. The chalked number six on the side of the hull is the method that we used to identify the models.

at the top. These masts became shorter and thinner in section as they went upwards. All of the sections had a slight taper with the thickest part being the closest to the deck. The lower mast had a D-shaped platform, known as a 'top', a few feet under its intersection with the topmast. In the Hornblower series this is referred to as a fighting top. This was also the area where the topmast overlapped the lower mast for added strength and the topmast slotted into the trestles which supported the top. The topmast was prevented from toppling by the cap which was

Looking down onto the deck of the 74-gun ship HMS *Justinian*. This was one of the most detailed models built for the series, but compromises still had to be made. This type of ship should have an open weather deck between the fore and main mast and not be flush decked as can be seen in this view. This false deck was easily lifted off using the square holes – just visible where the gangways would be across the waist of the deck. One of the models of the *Julia* is in the background.

tennoned at the top of the lower mast, and then it passed through a hole in the forward part of the cap. The fighting top was used by seamen working on the rigging and also acted as a spreader for the standing rigging for the topmast. On a warship, marines would be stationed on the fighting top during action with muskets and a swivel gun to sweep the enemy's deck when in close action. Just below the top of the topmast were the trestles – these had a similar function to the fighting top but did not carry a deck. Above this was the topgallant which ended in a button upon which was a pulley used for pulling up flags from the deck.

Attached to each section of the mast was a yard, of which there were usually three, although at this period it was also common to have four. The yards became smaller in length and section the higher they were up the masts. Starting at the bottom, the sails were named after the mast which they belonged to. For example, the mainmast's sails were the main course, main top, topgallant and at the very top, the royal. The bowsprit was constructed in a similar way to the masts but unlike the masts its heel was not mounted on the keelson but seated on heavy timbers; these were downward extensions of the bitts in front of the foremast. There were various other ways of securing the bowsprit but this was the most common method, and would have been used on the real ship types appearing in Hornblower. Again the *Julia* was the exception, because she was of a design which was over one hundred years later than the Hornblower period.

Masts were always made from some kind of fir and imported mainly from the Baltic and Canada. Fir was the most suitable timber for mast construction because it was obtainable in long lengths which were mostly free from knots, shakes and other blemishes. A small mast could be fashioned from a single tree and was called a pole mast. The mast was built around a central spindle and side trees, side fishes, cheeks and front fishes were added to this; these were then intricately spliced and coaked together, finally being secured by bolts and iron bands.

As can be seen from the brief description above, masts are more complex in construction than they first appear. From a distance the lower masts look like round poles but closer inspection reveals them to be made from many parts. The visible part of the lower masts have two cheeks protruding from the outboard side of them, which adds strength. At the top they are cut away to act as a support for the trestles upon which the fighting top sits. Running down the forward part of the lower mast is the rubbing paunch, which looks like a batten of wood nailed along its length; its purpose was to protect the lower mast from flapping sails. All the upper masts and bowsprit are of a simpler construction, being mostly round in section except at their ends which are square or octagonal.

There could be as many as fifteen yards on a fighting warship excluding flagstaffs and studdingsail booms which would more than double that figure. Yards were constructed in a slightly different way. Starting from the centre of a yard, looking at it lengthways, the pole is octagonal and has two cleats which are for securing the jeer blocks (which support the yard when it is on the mast). Yards also have a parrel (which looks like a double necklace) fitted to the centre and its function is to hold the yard against the mast. The barrels of the necklace are free to run on their string, so they also act as a bearing when the yard, with sail attached, is rotated around the mast to catch the wind. The octagonal section runs approximately a quarter of the length before becoming rounded and tapered in section at its extremities; at the ends of most yards there is a slot into which a pulley wheel is fitted. I have given this very brief description of the main visible features of masts and yards to give the reader some appreciation of what had to be built for the eleven models.

It is by no means a full description of full-sized practice but the Hornblower models included all of the features mentioned above.

The model's masts and yards were very much simplified from full-sized practice. Many of the detailed fittings you would find on a model in a museum are only suggested or hinted at on the Hornblower models – a lot of this visual detail is of course not required for a TV film. All of the masts and yards on the models were constructed in a similar fashion. Starting with the overall dimensions of the particular yard or mast, thin planks of pine were cut to a thickness slightly wider than the yard or mast. A sufficient number of those planks were layered together to make a square section. In making a mast, there may be as many as six of these planks which were all glued and clamped together. Onto this square-sectioned billet the cheeks and hounds, which are the visible features, were marked out. Then came the labour intensive bit. The mast was hand planed into a rounded section along its length, judged by eye, and the shape of the cheeks were chiselled out down the sides. When the mast section or yard had been roughly chiselled, and planed to its final shape, the whole thing was sanded smooth. The batten on the front of the mast, if used, was glued and nailed to the front of it. The yards were much easier to make. The laminated billet of timber was planed octagonal at the centre of its length and the round taper for the remainder was shaped in a similar way. Again this was finished off with sandpaper. The making of the masts and yards occupied several men for many weeks. It is worth making the point here that the men who made all the small parts of the models worked in a freezing cold workshop with the simplest of hand tools and very poor lighting, probably in a similar way to the shipwrights who built the original ships. I had nothing but respect for their abilities under what were difficult conditions to say the least.

Most ships from the Napoleonic period had one to three masts plus a bowsprit. A mast is a vertical spar set into the ship, and its prime use was, of course, to carry sails. In the eighteenth-century nearly all of the major warships carried square sails which made them very efficient when the wind was behind them or a few points off the wind but, unlike a modern yacht they were less accomplished at going across the wind let alone into the wind. Consequently it was common for ships to have to wait for a favourable wind to take them in the required direction. Additionally, when the wind is very light a sailing warship needs every inch of sail it can put onto its masts and yards to make progress through the water. To this end extensions were attached to the yards (the crosspieces of timber which the sails hang from), which is called studdingsail and pronounced 'stunsail'. Studdingsails were attached to booms which slid out beyond the end of the yard in a telescopic fashion, effectively doubling the area of the sail. With a full set of these additional sails combined with normal sails, a ship could make progress even in a very light wind. After much discussion amongst the modelling team about the logistics of handling these extra booms and sails, it was decided to omit them from the models. It was felt that there were enough problems handling the other sails without the added complications that studdingsails would have presented.

The fighting tops were also made in this workshop, together with most of the other fittings. As I outlined earlier, a top is a 'D'-shaped platform with a planked deck on it – sitting on an 'H'-shaped trestle at the top of the lower mast. These were simplified by being made up of two or three planks of wood glued together, edge on, and then cut to shape on a bandsaw. The planking on its top surface was excluded, because it would never be seen by the camera. Some of the tops were cut out of appropriately thick plywood. The supporting 'H' trestle for the top was accurately simulated, because it would be seen along with the other trestle or 'crosstrees' at the top of the fore or main topmasts. These had holes drilled into them at their outboard edges to accept the deadeyes which are part of the standing rigging discussed in a later section.

Looking forward down the deck of the model HMS *Indefatigable*. The large pale flat area in the foreground is a hatch cover giving access to the interior of the hull.

The rigging

We have looked at the masts and yards, and seen how they were made for the models. To make the sails catch the wind and to support the various masts, a complex system of rigging was employed; it fell into two main types with very different functions. The 'standing rigging' was fixed and permanent and gave support to the masts, and transferred some of the pull from the sails down to the hull at the channels and deadeyes on the sides of the ship. It was easily differentiated from the 'running rigging' because it was coated in a tar based solution to give it protection from the elements. The running rigging can simply be decribed as any line which passes through a block (hence it has no tar on it) and is almost always a pale natural colour. If tar was applied to the running rigging it would have interfered with the working of the ship's sails.

In addition to the rigging there are hundreds of blocks needed to enable the running rigging to do its work of sail handling. For the Hornblower models, we needed thousands of blocks ranging in sizes from 19mm (0.75 inch) to 50mm (2 inches) long. Many had single and double pulley sheaves. There are many types of blocks to be found on a ship's rigging including violin, sister and ram's head to name just a few. For the Hornblower models we were faced with a problem – the model's rigging had to look realistic and convincing, but at the same time it had to be easy to work and indeed change for the various roles that the ships were to play. Part of the answer was to survey all of the models and come down to a manageable number of standard types of block which could be used on each of them. Eventually we arrived at four sizes of single blocks and two of doubles. The Russian builders proposed to make them all by hand from wood, but it was soon noted that wooden blocks swell when wet and this would have hindered their operation particularly since the blocks did not have pulley wheels in them, which would have helped the rope to run through. Their inclusion would have made manufacturing more expensive and very time consuming. It soon became obvious that a man working on his own could only produce a limited number of blocks in the time we had available. The solution was to cast the blocks in resin from silicone moulds. The materials for this process had to be imported from all over from England. Once I had made the moulds and show the man who was casting them how to mix the resin, complete with a brown dye to give them a wood colour, they were all produced within a couple of weeks - his speed of production only being limited by the curing time of the resin. The argument for this strategy was that it cost thirty dollars a week to pay a man to make blocks and the resin cost one hundred dollars for a gallon can of which many were needed for block making. Suffice to say the Hornblower production company provided the resin. Each time the mixed resin was poured into the moulds about twenty four different sized blocks were produced. When the blocks came out of the moulds they had to be separated from each other because the intergrated channel cut into the moulds to allow the resin to flow through it to form the blocks held them together. The moulded blocks required very little cleaning up afterwards and worked very satisfactorily.

The standing rigging needed many deadeyes and hearts which gave tension to the rigging and secured the masts in their upright position. The deadeyes were produced by an outside contracter on a CNC lathe using a fine grained oak. The hearts, which tension the stays on the forward part of the masts, were manufactured by hand from various types of hard wood. On some of the models, especially the French frigate, the back stays (which are behind the shrouds) we did not use deadeyes for tension, but used double and triple blocks instead. These were manufactured by hand because there were not a large number of them and they did not have the same operational requirements as the running rigging blocks. All of the fore and aft stays, which run along the centre of the ship up to the masts were made to be easily detached in a similar way to the deadeyes. This facilitated the removal of the masts. They had a simple tensioning screw at the lower end to give some slack, which was useful when the masts were re-erected in the preparation prior to filming.

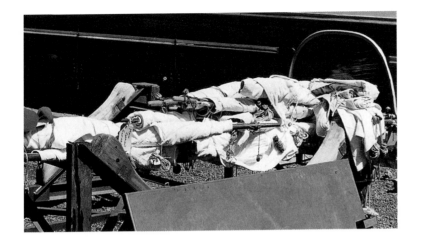

Some appreciation of what was involved to re-rig the models at Pinewood can be gained from this pile of sails, rigging and spars waiting to be sorted out and distributed to the appropriate model. There were some labels to help with identification but the original ones were in Russian and most of the interpreters I worked with did not have sufficient specialist knowledge of ship rigs to translate them into English

Each mast was inserted into the keelson with a locating rod and threaded bolt, complete with a metal plate screwed to the keelson to increase stability. The bolt had a nut and washer on it so that when the nut was rotated on the thread it gaves about 50mm (2 inches) of up and down movement to the mast. This was done so that when the standing rigging came to be re-erected and, with the nut previously slackened off, there was no tension on the standing rigging – making it easier to hook the deadeyes strops into the chains. After the mast and rigging were all in position, it was a simple matter to put a spanner on the nut and raise the mast 25mm (1 inch) or so and re-tension the standing rigging. Not all of the models had their masts set up on the keelson – some were set up

A close-up of the channels on one of the 4-metre frigates, giving an idea of how the dead eyes and shrouds are secured with a quick release mechanism.

Looking over the bows of the HMS *Indefatigable* towards the screen behind the tank, with two other models in the background.

on the deck and supported by the beams below using a similar system as fitted to the keelson. When the models were re-rigged at Pinewood after many weeks in transit it was found that the rigging had shrunk. This was rectified by releasing all the lanyards (pieces of rope inserted into the deadeyes to make the rigging taut) on the deadeyes and retensioning them in situ, a time consuming exercise.

The rigging itself was all assembled by a very experienced rigger called Victor, with the assistance of his apprentice. This team had rigged all of the Russian construction company's full-sized ships. Every process to do with the rigging was carried out in exactly the same way as in full-sized practice. This meant that all of the blocks were either spliced on to the end of the fall (the end of the rope which was pulled to create tension) or whipped with thin string in traditional fashion. When the rigging, which was mostly assembled off the models prior to fitting to the masts, was set up it all looked extremely neat and tidy without any obvious inconsistencies

Much debate took place as to what material should have been used for the rigging. Traditional materials like jute and hemp were considered until we realised that these materials swell and con-tract with changing weather conditions. Nylon rope was eventually chosen for all the rigging and it was required in huge quantities and of varying thickness. It was all sourced in various parts of Russia, and that required for the standing rigging to be hand dyed black. This process involved various mixtures and with varying degrees of success. At one point we had a coloured mixture which looked black in the mixing pot but when it was applied to the nylon rope a chemical reaction occured and turned the rope bright orange – far from the desired effect! The solution that did work was a mixture of what looked like Stockholm tar and black paint watered down with turpentine. I am often vague about formulas and processes which were used in the construction of the models because my interpreter frequently did not know what they were himself and often displayed a considerable lack of technical understanding.

The sails

The most visible part of any ship is her sails and we went to great lengths to ensure that they looked as realistic as possible. Various materials were considered with this criteria in mind. Many models, when fitted with sails, just do not look convincing and we wanted to overcome this problem. Modern spinnaker and sail cloth, canvasses, nylon, cotton and even dress making materials were contemplated. I experimented with these cloths down at the lakeside, soaking them to see how they behaved when wet and to see if they held the wind in a convincing way when wet or dry. Any passing local Russians must have thought that this Englishman had taken leave of his senses as I washed and held the various materials up in the wind to see how they behaved. They were either too light or heavy, did not hang convincingly, or exhibited other problems such as fraying. Many modern materials have some form of treatment applied to them which, when crumpled and then hung to look like a sail, look as though they need ironing – most unconvincing. Colour was important, and we hardly want the sails to look too much like freshly laundered bedsheets. All of the sail material was off white in colour; it was suggested by Andrew (the designer) at one point that we soak the finished sails in a cold tea solution, but this did not give the desired, realistic effect.

The models were split into two groups for sail making purposes – the large ones which needed a heavier material and the smaller ones required something much lighter so that the sails looked in scale. We could find nothing locally which satisfied us, so we referred the search task to the London office. After much searching, the props buyer came up with curtain lining material which is 50% cotton and 50% synthetic and calico for the smaller models and an artist's 8 ounce canvas for the larger ones. I got a much needed break returning to London to purchase the sail and other materials which were required yet unavailable in Russia.

The dictionary description of a sail is an assemblage of cloths of canvas, cut to the necessary length and fashioned to a particular shape which is designed to catch the wind and use its force to give motion to a sailing vessel; a real life sail is more complex than this. The cloths are stitched together with a double seam and the leech of the sail shaped with gores to give it the required aerodynamic curve. The Hornblower model's sails fall into two types – the square sails which are set on horizontal yards crossing the masts and the fore and aft sails set up on the stays which are variations on the triangular shape. The four sides of a square sail are the head (top), foot (bottom), and the two leeches (sides). The top two corners are the earing cringles, the bottom corners are the clews. Normally a sail is made up of strips of canvas running vertically, double stitched together and tailored to give a full belly which assists the sail to catch the wind. Around the edges of a sail is the bolt-rope stiched into the seam which added strength to it. On the upper parts of a sail are as many as three bands of reefing ropes used to shorten the sail in times

opposite page top

A deck view of HMS *Indefatigable* showing
the model's guns from the inboard side. When
the guns fired electronically, they recoiled with
the force of the explosion into
the black tubes which can be seen behind the
barrels. When reloading, the barrels would
be pulled to the run-out position.

opposite page bottom

The Ukrainian model film crew intended to fire
the model's cannons with a computerised control. The technicians at Pinewood simplified the
whole operation with this device, which looks
like a xylophone. To fire a model cannon, the
wooden handled pointer on the end of the wire
would be lightly brought into contact with one
of the strips on the 'xylophone'. All of the cannons could be fired at once by rapidly running
the pointer along its length, or a ragged broadside could be effected by randomly selecting
strips. This system is simple but very effective.

of higher wind velocities. The sail is attached to the yard by the cringles at its top corners and robands along its head which secure the sail to the yard. The stay sails are similar.

When looked at with a cursory glance the sails on the Hornblower models appear to be miniatures of full-size ones, complete with the strips stitched together as in the practice of full-sized ships. The individual sails were actually made up from one piece of material which had darts cut into the top and bottom along the line of the vertical seams to tailor the belly shape after it had been sewn together. All of the other details, including the bolt-rope around its edge, reefing bands, clews and cringles are all included. They differ from full-size sails in one area although the principle is the same – the head of the sail has boot lace eyes and instead of individual rabands for each eye they are laced onto the yard with a thin nylon cord. This was done to make sail fitting and removal a simpler and more rapid process than the normal practice of individual rabands.

The armament and fittings

A principal component of any sailing warship was its armament, be it for offensive or defensive purposes. In the eighteenth century the main artillery aboard ship was the muzzle-loaded carriage gun of which there were three types: the carriage gun used in the main battery, swivel guns mounted on strong timbers around the ship's rail and up in the fighting top, and finally the carronade (a shorter, lighter carriage gun used principally at close range) which had only recently been introduced. None of the Hornblower models carried any carronades because we simply did not have the time to produce them, and they would have been an added complication to an already complex situation during filming.

There were two types of cannon fitted to the Hornblower models. The small swivel guns, the main armament, were all non-working dummies and were complemented by the deck guns, of which there were two sets for each model. One set were dummies whilst the others fired a blank, electronically operated charge. The armament used on the Hornblower models was based upon several guns of the period. The type of gun they loosely resemble was a quarter deck 9-pounder from 1761, as found in contemporary warships such as the 74-gun ship HMS *Bellona*. Each model had its own complement of dummy and working cannon turned from wood on a CNC lathe by outside contractors. The detail was not complete along their length, but the muzzle and about half of its length was accurately copied; inside the ship's walls, the guns were simply black cylinders. This was the case on all the models with the exception of the 74-gun HMS *Justinian* (which had fully detailed cannons on its upper decks) because the rear part of the cannon would never be seen by the camera. The difference between the working cannon and the

dummies was that the working ones had a short metal cylinder fitted into the mouth of the muzzle. The back of the metal cylinder was blanked off and a 'V'-shaped wire heating element fitted into it facing towards the gun's muzzle. Behind the element were wires which led out through a hole in the back of the cannon to the switch which fed the 12 volts of electrical current required to fire the gun. To load the cannon, a small cylindrical paper cartridge, which had been made up beforehand by the operator, was pushed gently down onto the element in the cannon's muzzle, which, because of its 'V'-shape, penetrated the back of the paper cartridge and engaged the small amount of gunpowder inside. When an electrical charge was applied to the element it ignited the powder which fired the gun. The carriages for all of the cannon barrels were securely mounted onto a simplified version of a real one, but without its wheels and detailing. They were secured to the deck with heavy rubber bands made from cut up bicycle inner tubes. The barrel of the gun, when fired, recoiled into a spring-loaded metal tube mounted on the carriage. The tube into which the barrel fitted was securely mounted onto the carriage with a light, long spring inside abutted to the back of the wooden barrel. To reload the barrel, it was withdrawn from the tube, any debris from the previous firing was cleaned out and a fresh paper cartridge was fitted into the muzzle ready for another firing. It took about ten minutes to reload each model's battery of cannons.

A ship has numerous deck fittings, many of which were made for the models. The criteria applied to work out if a particular fitting was made was if the particular fitting could be seen from a rowing boat standing approximately 20-30 metres (66-98 feet) away from a real ship. If so it was included in the inventory.

Looking aft along the deck of the 4-metre frigates giving an indication of the level of detail included on the models.

Bitts, the wheel and the davits (wooden frames for storing spare booms and spars) are highly visible, as are all external features of the hull. A full complement of anchors were made for each model which, when in position on the fore channels, are a highly-visible feature at the bow of a ship. Most ships of this period had at least four anchors of a similar pattern; during the Napoleonic wars the Royal Navy mostly used Bower type anchors, which were made of wrought iron with a wooden stock. These could weigh several tons on a large warship and were a considerable achievement of the smith's art of the period. The anchors on the models were only there as dressing so they were made of wood in either pine or birch. The metal parts of the anchors were jointed together and the stock was shaped from a solid – unlike under the traditional method where the stock would be made in two halves. The flukes of the anchors were sometimes made of plywood or pine with the largest anchors made for the models were nearly 122cm (4 feet) high with the smaller ones being about 45cm (18 inches).

Each model had a binnacle – which again is a highly visible piece of furniture – situated in front of the ship's wheel so that the helmsman can easily see it

The double wheel of the *Grand Turk*.
Although the ship could be steered from this
wheel – most of the steering was done from
an imitation eighteenth-century binnacle box
which has a sophisticated computer-controlled
hydraulic system installed.

when he is standing his spell at the wheel. It consists of a box with draws in the top with three glazed windows below. The central window has a lamp in it, to illuminate the compass at night, with a chimney on top. A compass is situated on either side, so if the helmsman is on one side of the wheel he always has sight of a compass to maintain his course. The model's binnacles are all solid wood with a few of the main features glued onto the outside. Some of the Russian workers got quite carried away and produced a lot more detail on this feature than was actually required.

All of the models had a wheel which was sawn from a piece of plywood. The turned spikes on some of these were dowels slid into pre-drilled holes around the rim, secured at the hub in the centre. Some of the models had quite highly finished wheels, because the workman took both these and some other parts home to work on.

Most of the models had capstans which were made up in block form from pine. They did not have any capstan bars although the sockets into which these would fit were suggested in simple form. The capstan was used for the heavy lifting work on board a ship – this included lifting the anchors, guns, ship's boats and yards. The crew, sometimes four abreast, walked around the capstan pushing on the bars which provided the muscle power to do this heavy work. Some of the smaller frigates and fireships had a windlass fashioned from a solid piece of wood. All of these parts, although looking realistic, would not stand up to close scrutiny. At the break of the forecastle most ships of this period had a belfry. These made an interesting visual feature and so they were included on the Hornblower models.

Food was prepared and cooked in the galley, which was usually situated under the forecastle in an eighteenth-century warship. The cooking was usually supervised by a retired or invalid sailor and his assistants. The cook presided over a

The quarter galleries of the *Grand Turk*.

large stove which had various compartments within it.

Most of the food was boiled in two large kettles built into the top of it; in its sides were ovens and at the front was a grill. All these features cannot be seen from the outside and the only visible part being the chimney which protrudes above the deck just behind the foremast. The chimney could be rotated to take the fumes away from the ship in the wind and was made of metal. All of the model's chimneys were carved from wood.

Various hatches, covered with gratings, were situated along the centre-line of a ship's decks. Their main purpose is to give ventilation and access to the lower decks and holds. The gratings are jointed together and are very time consuming to make. They lie in a coaming which is higher than deck level to prevent any water from the deck going down into the main body of the ship. For the purpose of the models, gratings and their coamings were only fitted to the poop and forecastle decks. The ventilation holes, which are usually square, were drilled into plywood to represent these openings. Various other features were included on the model's decks, including bitts around the masts where the running rigging was belayed. Thousands of turned scale wooden belaying pins were then attached to the rails on the models. The pins were contracted out of the yard to a company who had a Computer Numerically Controlled (CNC) lathe. On the fireship models, which were the first to be built and completed, the pins were carved by hand but this proved to be to slow a method considering the thousands which had to be made in various sizes. They also looked very crude, but thankfully they are difficult to see on the screen.

A very notable feature on the upper decks of ships from this period is the boat tier. A frigate may carry as many as five of these boats on a skid beams spanning the well deck just in front of the main mast. These were not used as lifeboats as on a modern ship; in a sailing ship the ship's boats had many uses. Compared with a modern ship, most warships of this period

The small rowing boat used by Hornblower to board a fireship to steer it away from a fiery grave, and therefore save HMS *Indefatigable*.

rarely came into a harbour except for maintenance and major overhauls, so the crew, stores and water were rowed out to the ships at their anchorage. The most well known anchorages were Spithead and the Nore (in the east Solent and mouth of the river Thames respectively) but there were many others around the coast of Britain. The ships could be anchored several miles off shore as in the case of the young Hornblower being taken to the 74-gun ship HMS *Justinian* in the opening scene of the first episode of the television series. The ship was anchored at Spithead waiting to be sent off on her next commission.

In normal practice, a ship carried three boats stowed abreast across the beams; to save space, the smaller boats were stowed inside the largest. The largest boats used were launches; these had originally been dockyard craft, but were standardised for use by the Royal Navy in the 1780s and were used to carry heavy weights such as fresh water barrels. A slightly longer launch, known as the pinnace or barge, was used as the admiral's or captain's transport between ship and shore. Much time and energy was expended on the care and presentation of these boats and in certain cases they could be quite garishly painted. Wealthy captains often spent significant sums of money on the uniforms of the boats' crew as they were, in effect, a visible extension of the ship's reputation.

As so many ship's boats were needed for the models, some degree of standardisation was required. To this end three different sizes were made, which would be used on all the models regardless of scale. They were made off-site in Kiev, by a vacuum forming process. Vacuum forming is a technique where a plastic sheet material is heated until it reaches a floppy and elastic state and then it is sucked, using a vacuum pump, down onto a former – which in this case was the shape of the boat – and allowed to cool. When cool it is removed from the former, leaving a simple trimming exercise to remove the excess from the original sheet. This was a quick and easy solution to the problem of the boats. Unfortunately, I do not remember these boats often being on-screen during the series. This is most easily explained because most of the scenes are of the ships in action, and when a ship was in action it was common practice to either tow the boats behind the ship or tie them together and temporally abandon them for collection when the action had ended. This was done as their position on the ship's deck exposed them to enemy cannon fire and if hit whilst on the deck, they produced flying wooden splinters which would cause unnecessary casualties.

Around the bulwarks of a ship, there are many bollards used as belaying points for various parts of the rigging; they are also convenient anchorage points for ropes during various ship handling operations. All of the models had a full complement of them. Hammock nettings proved to be a real problem, as they are highly visible; it was normal practice when the crew woke up in the morning for them to roll their hammocks up and stow them in the 'U'-shaped troughs running around the side of the ship. This was a convenient place to stow the hundreds of hammocks which were aboard a ship and they additionally afforded extra protection to the crew from small arms fire and splinters, and also made it difficult for enemy boarders to gain access to the deck. There is some conjecture that if Nelson had allowed the hammock nettings to be increased in height on HMS *Victory*, the sharpshooter in the mast of the *Redoubtable* at the battle of Trafalgar might not have found him such an easy target. Behind the nettings were wooden rails, especially on the poop deck; these were the most noticeable feature of the models since the nettings were rarely used. The nettings proved to be a nuisance during filming because

opposite page

The first model to be launched , the English frigate, was assisted into the water by many willing hands. The model had very little ballast in it – which helped in the launching operation. On the far right is the over-taxed Andrew Mollo, overseeing the operation and probably sighing with relief after all the delays and problems he had experienced could be set aside, watching one of the models going into the water ready for filming.

they were always where a man needed to put his feet when loading the cannon or working on the rigging or sails. They were used mostly on HMS *Justinian*, but are rarely to be seen on the other models for this reason.

The nettings would have been difficult to make if we had adhered to traditional practice, where long barricades of netting are tied together in diamond formation. The problem was ingeniously resolved by Micky Spence, the plasterer on the production team. His suggestion was to make up a board with nails spaced at the apex of the diagonals then run string soaked in resin between the nails to make the familiar netting pattern. When the resin had set the joins were all stuck together by the overlapping string forming the net. An added feature of this method was that the nettings were stiff and waterproof which meant they would not sag and look untidy.

Painting

The colour schemes of the models are given in the later ship-by-ship reference section (see pages 89 and 94). As I mentioned earlier, when construction had been completed the hull of each model was given a coat of varnish or preservative along with its masts and spars. There was, however, still a lot of work to be done before the models could be put in front of the camera. The first task was to mask all of the imperfections with waterproof car body filler and then rub it down by hand or with palm sanders. At first it was suggested that we painted them using Rosco concentrated water based paints, which is used extensively in the film industry; we did this until it was discovered that the substance came off when exposed to water. After this experience the models were all painted using oil-based enamels and gloss paint which are more familiar to ship modellers. To take off the shine from these paints two strategies were used – the addition of the undercoat to gloss and enamel dulled the shine to a flat sheen. If it was still too shiny, a coat of matt varnish was applied. A matt finish is essential on anything put in front of a camera, because once bright lights are applied there is a considerable danger of an on-screen flare effect from the shine; a matt finish also enhances the illusion that the model is bigger than it really is.

Inside the tank compound at Polikur Studios. The Spanish frigate, on the left, is in the state in which the ships were delivered from the workshops in Petrozavodsk. All of the painting was done near to the filming site so that any last minute changes could be taken into account. On the right is the English frigate with its painting complete, waiting for its masts and rigging to be erected.

2. The models in use

A faint black cloud was just visible between the schooner's masts. It thinned again, and Bush could not be perfectly sure. The nearest gun bellowed out, and a chance flaw of wind blew the powder smoke about them as they stood together, blotting out their view of the schooner. "Confound it all!" said Bush, moving about restlessly in search of a better viewpoint.
The other guns went off almost simultaneously and added to the smoke.

Lieutenant Hornblower

The first Hornblower model to be put into the water was on the tank at Yalta, which had been specially constructed for the models to be filmed in. I contributed nothing to the planning or construction of the tank, all the building work having been completed whilst I was in Petrozavodsk. In the end only fifteen scenes were actually filmed in the Yalta tank, which I am given to understand cost some £50,000 to build, a considerable financial investment by the Hornblower production company for so small a return of fifteen scenes out of the eventual one hundred and fifty required. The greater proportion of the model scenes were filmed at Pinewood Studios the following year, due to considerable technical difficulties and other irresolvable problems at Yalta. The Yalta tank was also intended to be used for other non-model scenes in the series, such as when Hornblower is being towed behind HMS *Indefatigable* with one of his seaman. This was done in the tank at Pinewood, as were some other scenes which used the large rowing boats. This chapter explores how the now completed models were put to use at both Yalta and Pinewood, the technical aspects of filming and special effects together with an explanation of how some of the larger sets and equipment were employed to create the films.

The Models at Yalta and Pinewood

Looking from above, the shape of the two tanks used for the filming of the models resembles a straight sided fan. I will give details of the tank built in Yalta first because, although their design principle is the same, the methods and approaches used for the filming were significantly different.

The tank at Yalta is situated in Polikur studios, on a hill overlooking the city on one side and the vast expanse of the Black Sea on the other. The short end of the tank looks out towards the sea and this is where the camera was situated, on

A happy Ukrainian film crew – full of champagne – filling the newly launched model with ballast to keep it upright. The shallow depth of the water can be appreciated when one realises that the men are standing on the bottom of the tank. This picture was taken after the sides of the tank were raised to make it deeper.

a concrete apron with its attendant camera men, director and crew. At the long end, furthest away from the camera, the walls of the tank were slightly lower in height, allowing the water to overflow into a trough behind. The lip over which the water flowed was painted silver in colour, so that the lip and the natural sea beyond became merged, thus giving the illusion that the scene taking place in the tank was being recorded at sea, complete with a natural horizon. This type of tank is consequently described as a 'horizon tank'. The overflow water, in the trough, was pumped back into the tank at a point which was out of view of the camera. Standing at the camera position it was possible to see the sea beyond and its horizon with the sky above. This illusion worked fairly well but, as can be seen from some of the photographs in this book, the line between the tank's edge and the sea beyond was very noticeable when the camera angle was high in relation to the tank's water level. When the filming was in progress, the camera was mounted on a cantilever beam and lowered as close to the water as was practical.

The construction of the tank at Yalta was a large engineering project, into which considerable thought and money was invested. The Yalta tank was intended as a long term investment which was to be used for the first four episodes and the intended subsequent series of Hornblower films. In the event, it was only used for a small number of scenes in the first two episodes and not all of these were actually used in the final production. The Yalta shots are easily identified because they have a beautiful blue sky with thin, elevated white clouds. The site on which the tank was built had to be cleared and then levelled, to ensure that the weight of the water in the finished tank would be evenly spread. A layer of soft sand was laid over the bedrock and earth, as a protective foundation for the relatively fragile butyl rubber tank liner. This liner was used to contain the water rather like a giant pond. The tank itself was approximately eighty feet wide at its most extended point and about fifty feet from the camera to the overflow lip. The depth of water in the tank as built was approximately 76cm (30 inches). The sides of the tank were made up in right-angled triangular sections of welded girders, with sheet steel welded to the triangles to form a shallow slope to the bottom. This slope also made it easier for the crew to enter the water to work on the models. I believe that this configuration was arrived at to give maximum strength to the sides which held back the considerable weight of many tons of water. To ensure that the tank was water tight, wide strips of the butyl rubber liner were laid over the sand base and up the sides of the tank. A specialist was flown from England to carefully bond these strips together to make the tank water tight. To protect the fragile butyl rubber bottom from heavy keels of the models (as well as people's feet), a layer of soft sand was poured onto the floor of the tank before it was filled with water. Unsurprisingly it took an entire week to fill this vast tank with fresh water.

The butyl rubber liner was thankfully made oversized, which later allowed us to increase the depth of the tank. The water's depth was the result of a misunderstanding between the English production company and the Ukrainian film crew director of models, Velodia Maluik (who was employed on the strength of his con-

The fireship set after filming, complete with fire damage around the gunports. In the foreground the water tank may clearly be seen giving the impression that the set is afloat on the sea. Note the gunports are hinged to open downwards, allowing the flames from the combustible load to be fed with fresh air.

siderable experience filming models for a French film called 'Captain Blood'). All of the model sequences filmed on that picture had been conducted on the open sea, with all of the props and scenery being set up either on the shore side or on floating barges. The original intention was to employ similar techniques for a number of shots in the Hornblower films, but as the filming commenced the decision was taken to film all of the models in the tank. The reason for this, as explained to me, was that filming models in the open sea would be very time-consuming and the transportation of all of the equipment to an open sea location would be unnecessarily expensive, not to mention the problems created in handling and controlling very large models in an open sea environment. Velodia had originally surveyed the plans of the models and intended to film the smaller ones in the tank and the larger in the open sea; he had therefore ordered the tank to be built so that only the smaller models needed to float comfortably in it. As it transpired, even they would have had their keels rubbing along the bottom, and as a result the sides of the tank were raised in height by about 15cm (6 inches) to give 91cm (3 feet) of water depth. This was still not really deep enough to be used effectively in the way that the production required. How were we to sink a model ship in water only three feet deep when the model's hull alone was nearly four feet high? These problems which we avoided by deciding not to film at sea in turn created additional headaches which needed to be overcome.

A great deal of equipment and skilled manpower is required to film models for TV production. Camera or cameras, wind machines, a crane (for lifting the model in and out of the water), smoke machines, various types of explosives for special effects, and many other pieces of equipment have to be readily available. To operate all of these different facets, an experienced body of crew with varying skills is required. Some of the tasks which had to be completed before filming could begin included positioning the models, setting sails, loading model cannons, and the positioning of wind machines in conjunction with any special effects smoke. This could

A general view of the tank area at Polikur studios. On the right is the Ukrainian wind machine – an old propeller-driven Yak fighter mounted on a farm cart – to fill the model's sails with wind. This device was noisy, very clumsy and difficult to use. In the background the English frigate can be seen floating on the tank, with a natural wind filling its sails.
In the far background are some old sets from another film. The two men in the centre are part of the English production team.

take a considerable time to prepare before an inch of film could even run through the camera. On Hornblower, the entire team had to additionally combat the problem caused by the language barrier together with the clash of techniques and approaches which different people used to solve our problems.

The schedule which had been drawn up for the Ukrainian model film unit was to shoot five scenes a day. At first sight this does not seem too unreasonable, allowing for all of the models and equipment being in the right place at the right time; but invariably this is not how it happened. After I left Petozavodsk to come down to Yalta, the company who constructed them started to deliver the models late. The locally supplied equipment which was required to film the models was also often delivered late, and when it did arrive it was usually so old or problematic that it broke down before it could be commissioned. A good case in point was the crane built at Yalta Studios which was essential for lifting the models in and out of the tank. It was delivered late and when we tried to use it the gear box (which was

This tranquil looking pond is where all the model action took place at Pinewood. Four wind machines are waiting to be manoeuvred into position.

intended to rotate the crane on its base with a model suspended in its cradle) irreparably broke down and rendered the crane virtually useless. Wind machines were provided by the production team but the spark plugs fouled through incorrect use and these were also taken out of commission for several days while it was repaired. A makeshift wind machine was then introduced; it was formed from the forward fuselage of a wartime Yakovlev fighter, complete with engine and propeller. This machine proved to be very difficult to direct because the whole unit had to be wheeled around on a converted farm cart and did not allow the usual vertical movement. These are just a few examples of the difficulties faced by the crew at Yalta. The clock was ticking on the production, and the decision to move to the more advanced and established Pinewood facility came as a relief to many.

The tank at Pinewood Studios is situated behind the sound stages in a secluded area surrounded by trees. I gather it was built in 1958 and has been used for many well known films. The first thing that comes to your notice as you approach the Pinewood tank is an 18 metre (60 feet) high by 67 metre (220 feet) wide canvas screen stretched over a steel gantry which runs behind the tank. This screen was painted a light grey blue and would be the background sky for all of the scenes featuring the models. The purpose built tank at Pinewood, while not being the largest in the world (that accolade belongs to the Titanic tank used for the filming of the film of the same name), is still awesome to behold. The water is 1 metre (3 feet) deep with an area in the middle which is 2.8 metres (9 feet) deep, and for our purposes was ideal for the sinking of models. The water is contained by reinforced concrete walls about 1.3 metres (4.5 feet) high. Before the tank was filled with water it required a great deal of preparation; the tank is in more or less constant use by the film world and before the Hornblower models could be floated the tank had to be cleaned and all of the equipment which would be used during the filming had

Top left

The sterns of HMS *Justinian* (left) and HMS *Indefatigable* in the tank at Pinewood. The rope coming down the side of *Justinian*'s hull to the rudder would have been used in times of emergency, when the ships steering gear was put out of action by enemy gunfire or bad weather. Such tackles were commonly found on warships from this period.

top right

Looking at the overflow lip at the back of the tank at Pinewood. The water level would be raised sufficiently to flow over the lip to give the effect of an artificial horizon seen against the back screen (top left). The black pipe is part of the water circulating system. The two white pipes were pumped full of smoke during filming which would escape through tiny holes, giving the impression of clouds or fog, depending on the desired effect.

Some of the equipment used in the tank at Pinewood. The water is a metre deep which means that the tractor has been modified by raising its body to work in deep water. This machine was used for moving models and equipment around the tank. The petrol-driven wind machine (left) would be moved around with the tractor.

to be positioned ready for use. A small harbour area was created so that the models could be worked on before their debut in front of the camera. A tractor with a heightened wheel base became an essential piece of equipment and was used to tow or push the various steel walk ways from which the crew operated the wind machines and cameras without getting their feet wet. Mobile scaffold towers on wheels were also installed so that the rigging and sails on the models were easily accessible. Electric and petrol driven wind machines were set up on their own little mobile islands. A small fibreglass rowing boat, complete with outboard motor, was on call for unforeseen eventualities. Outside the tank, a small village of mobile buildings appeared – one for refreshments, another fitted out with video monitors to view the previous days rushes (quickly edited previews of the scenes filmed), and so on. A van for the camera crew was present and a small well equipped workshop for all the minor modifications which the models would require during the filming was also set up. A generator hummed quietly to itself while it provided the enormous amount of electricity needed to drive the lights and wind machines.

Filming the Hornblower series

Storyboards are used to give the director some indication of how to set up the camera, or cameras, for each individual scene and gives some indication of what the sets and props are to look like. Each scene is given a number code which is used for reference in editing. A film is rarely shot in the sequence which you will see it on the

Every sequence seen on the screen is planned beforehand, and to give the director and film crew some indication of what is wanted, comic strip style story boards are drawn. Camera angles and movements are shown, as well as the scene number, to help the film makers arrange the set and anything else which will be seen.

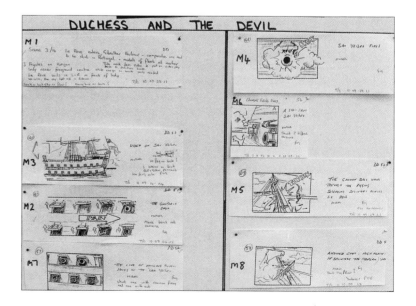

screen; the reason for this being that the particular set may be seen at the beginning of a film and reappear several times throughout. It therefore makes sense to film all the scenes using the set sequentially saving time and releasing the set building crew to build another set while the filming is taking place. Included in the storyboards were the model and full-sized ship sequences which had to be sorted out in a way which was clear to both the film director and the model director. Many of the scenes in which the models feature are intercut with the 'live action' (with actors), and the model sequences have to fit into the broader scheme seamlessly. In the first Hornblower episode, 'Even Chance', when Captain Pellew says the "French are coming out!" and turns to look at the French ships, those ships are models filmed at Pinewood, whilst the actor's shot was filmed in Yalta.

Shooting a scene may be done very quickly – in half an hour if it is a simple one. A more complicated scene may involve many people from many disciplines for many hours. Most of the shots with the models involved the incorporation of lots of smoke to simulate gun smoke, give the effect of a mist or fog, or (as in most shots) to soften the hard edge of the horizon so it will match the live action shots when intercut later. To simulate the motion of the sea powerful wind machines were directed down onto the water to create small waves. However if this was not done carefully, the end result could be 'shiny' waves which, to the camera's merciless lens, can look very artificial; this is often seen in earlier films, particularly those of the 1950s. The desired effect on the water is a matt appearance; this looks very convincing but takes time to set up correctly, involving a great deal of communication between the wind machine technicians and the model director. Once the water is looking as it should the model's sails need to be filled with wind to make it appear as if it is sailing, and not being dragged through the water on the end of cable attached to a towing tractor out of shot! The model's cannons, loaded previously, have to go off at the exact moment the model has gathered enough speed to have a convincing bow wave to the all-seeing camera. If there are two models in the shot then the problems are of course doubled. The other model may have to have explosives installed to simulate the damage from the incoming cannon fire, together with smoke and debris all carefully orchestrated and choreographed by technicians through visual judgement and contact via walkie-talkie. Wind machines roar, explosions flash, smoke billows everywhere, and then "Cut!" – it is all over. One single shot took about fifteen seconds, maybe a little less for simple ones. On the screen it seems to take significantly longer, since the whole action is recorded on an adjusted camera which records at six times normal speed. It is then played back at normal speed giving the illusion that the waves are moving like big ocean rollers and the model is proceeding in a leisurely fashion into action.

There were many different model scenes to be filmed for the Hornblower series, and thankfully not all of them included cannon fire. The *Julia* model playing the *Marie Galante* had to be seen to be sinking on film after the saturated rice had expanded and burst her underwater planking. This scene was understandably prepared weeks before the actual shoot date. A hydraulically-operated steel rig was made

above

Smoke still hangs in the air from an earlier sequence as the divers move in to manoeuvre the models into position for the next shot. The lanterns on the models are lit ready for a night scene to be filmed. HMS *Indefatigable* (closest to the camera) and HMS *Justinian* (behind *Indefatigable*), can be seen along with two 4-metre frigates in the background.

top

On the left, technicians generate smoke and direct it towards the obscured model being filmed. The two models on the far side of the tank are there for background interest during this shot. This picture gives a good indication of size of the background painted screen behind the tank.

above

Poor *Julia* taking a rest, lying slightly drunkenly in the water after having been sunk several times in one afternoon. The reason behind this was that she was not actually floating, but was being held up by a steel hydraulic rig beneath the water in the deep part of the tank. This rig was installed before the tank was filled with water.

top

The cameraman and model director at work filming a scene at Pinewood. In the foreground is *Julia*'s deck. Models in background from left to right: 4-metre frigate behind mast, Spanish frigate, HMS *Indefatigable* and an English frigate in Spanish colours.

in the workshops at Pinewood (it looked like a hydraulically-operated underwater robot with two arms which were attached to the models keel). This machine could roll the model onto its side, raise it, and lower it under the water. The model was prepared by having all of its ballast removed; this could be removed as the model no longer needed to float upright since this was now done by the rig. Compressed air pipes were fed to the tank floor under where the model was to sink. On the command of "Action!" the model rolled to one side and descended majestically into the deep, complete with mushrooms of bubbles bursting out of the sinking hull. This scene was shot eight times in an afternoon. On one occasion everything had gone as planned until the cameraman looked up and said, "What are those white things coming up with the debris?" White plastic cups which had been dropped into the model by careless onlookers. That shot was never shown!

The Gironde estuary was recreated in painted hardboard with model cannon firing to simulate the battery firing on HMS *Indefatigable*. Gibraltar's famous rock was recreated in a similar way. The Spanish merchant ship (which was specially built for this scene) is driven on to a specially built set of the Devil's Teeth for the episode, The 'Duchess and the Devil'. Close ups of the forward part of HMS *Justinian* were filmed at Pinewood using the model 74-gun, which was never designed to be seen that close, but after dressing looked very convincing.

Of course the model ships were not the only sets to be used in the production of Hornblower. Many different types of sets were developed and constructed for various scenes. The Lamb Inn and the surrounding streets of Portsmouth were built in the back lots of Yalta studios. The snow covered jetty on which Hornblower lands was a 'dressed' mole at Artek harbour, a few miles outside of Yalta. A local Crimean palace and its gardens were used for Hornblower's examination to become a lieutenant. This gives just a few examples of the many differing locations and sets used. The fireship sequence is a combination of model shots and a purpose-built set which is a life-size section of the ship.

Most of the scenes filmed aboard ships were either on the upper decks of the *Grand Turk* (playing HMS *Indefatigable*), or on a very large set which was known to the film crew as the 'pontoon', but in reality was a specially-built section of the 74-gun ship HMS *Justinian*, which takes a prominent role in the first episode of the series. A good number of the lower deck scenes, including those in the midshipman's quarters, the officer's wardroom, and lower gun deck were filmed on this large floating set. Hornblower's first experience onboard a warship in the first episode was filmed on the upper deck of the pontoon. It was an ex-Russian Navy pontoon originally used to service their Black Sea fleet, with a full-sized replica of a 74-gun, two-decked eighteenth-century warship built onto it. The interior and exterior were a close reproduction of the starboard (right) side of such a ship. It included the lower sections of the mizzen and main mast and its height, excluding the supporting structure for the rigging, rose from just below the waterline to a few feet above the dead-eyes anchoring the shrouds to the channels.

Built in a restricted military area of Sevastopol harbour by a Ukrainian set construction crew, the supporting framework was made up of shaped and welded steel girders with pine cladding fixed to it to give the desired effect and form. At this stage it had no paint, props or guns aboard and looked very clean and bright in the sunshine. Later, I spent quite a lot of time onboard this set helping in a small way to dress it. It was towed by a tug along the coast to Artek harbour, where the full-sized ships used in the production were based. It arrived unpainted and without any rigging or loose fittings (which included hammocks, buckets, gun equipment and the myriad of other flotsam and jetsam which go into the dressing of a set for filming); this all had to be added upon arrival at Artek. I have not included in this brief description any details of the lighting, cameras and other equipment which were brought into the area of the set for filming.

The deck of the pontoon looking aft towards the poop deck. The painting is complete and the set is mostly dressed, ready for filming. All that is missing is the crew and the personal items which will bring the set to life. Horatio Hornblower had his lessons in mathematics on this deck. The doors at the back of the set under the break of the poop open but lead nowhere.

The amount of work required to build the pontoon set brought home to me how much effort would have been involved in building the original warships with only simple hand tools, instilled an even greater respect within me for the eighteenth-century craftsman who built them. The pontoon may have been about a fifth of the length of an actual 74-gun ship and just over half of the original's deck width, complete with all of the deck fittings that would be found on the upper deck of a warship. Even so, standing beside the wheel and looking through the lower shrouds of the main mast over the starboard side with the sea beyond, it was not difficult to imagine myself standing in a similar position two hundred years ago. Looking down the quarter deck, with the ship's wheel behind me and belfry above on the poop deck, I could see four carriage guns at their ports with the main mast and bitts at the base. Beyond this the illusion was shattered as the deck abruptly came to an end with a modern safety rail to prevent the workers falling two decks down to the level of the lower gun deck. The illusion returned after descending the companion ladder behind the quarter deck grating to the lower gun deck. Lit only by the sun shining weakly through the grating above, the guns appeared out of the gloom at their closed ports and there was a sense of movement from the sea below. The equipment for firing the guns was all in place, including rammers, shot garlands and a human touch had been added by the hammocks, which swung gently from the deck head. The reason for the interior looking so convincing was the black screens placed all around to stop the light coming in during filming, hiding the modern clutter beyond.

The pontoon had been built with the model of HMS *Justinian* as the prototype and the model and the set had to visually match each other. When I had first

An exterior view of the pontoon set showing the side ladders which the young Midshipman Hornblower climbed up for his first sea posting. At the bottom left, some of the planking has been damaged and is waiting to be repaired after a recent storm.

seen the design drawings of the set in the Hornblower office in London, it was envisaged to be much bigger in size, including part of the well deck with the back end of the ship's boats sitting on their skid beams. The poop deck was also intended to be part of the set. This idea was considered too expensive and the set was redrawn much smaller, which explains why the camera is never seen to pan around the upper deck of the set during the films. There is one shot of the fore deck of HMS *Justinian* when Hornblower arrives on the ship; this shot was actually filmed on the model at Pinewood.

All of the main guns on the pontoon were designed to work, although they were never seen in action on this set because that was not part of the story line. There were many full-sized guns made for the production and they were all constructed in the Ukraine except the 32-pounders found on the lower gun deck, which were supplied by Martin Bibbins from the Trafalgar Gun Company. The full-sized Hornblower guns were cast at the naval yards at Sevastopol. Ship's guns of the past were cast whole from iron but the Hornblower guns were cast around a Katyshka rocket tube in sections of aluminium. The casting of the guns in aluminium was done on the advice of the people at the naval yard who normally cast parts for the ex-Soviet Navy's ships. It was realised that aluminium is not really suitable for ship's

HMS *Indefatigable* in action with a Spanish frigate.

guns and they suggested casting the rocket tubes into the guns to act as a strong barrel capable of taking the extreme pressure from exploding gun powder. Casting the guns in aluminium considerably reduced the guns weight when compared to an iron barrel, thus making them easier to transport and giving the extras, who would work them, a much lighter task. Unfortunately the standard rocket tube was not long enough to run the whole length of the gun, so several sections of the tube were welded together before casting. I watched the test firing of these guns next door to the model tank at Yalta and within a very short space of time Richard Rutherford Moore (the film unit's armourer) and Derek Langley (responsible for special effects) had blown off the back ends of these guns with a reduced charge of gun powder. The guns were sent back for more work to be administered. They were used in the production and can be seen in action on the decks of HMS *Indefatigable* in several scenes.

Richard Rutherford Moore and Martin Bibbins spent many hours next to the filming tank on a waste piece of ground, training the Ukrainian extras the art of firing two ship's guns. To aid them a mock up of two gun ports like those on the ships had been built, complete with enough wooden deck to give the illusion of being aboard a ship. They used modern replicas of all of the equipment which would

Looking down on the deck of the Spanish 4-metre frigate, showing the effects of having been badly blackened and burnt in action. The hanging sail can be seen to have some scorching.

be needed to service and fire the guns. I found this fascinating because I was watching a process which any gunner from Nelson's navy would have found familiar, despite the two hundred years' gap between us. Here was a collection of raw recruits without any previous knowledge of the art in which they were being trained being shown in easy stages a forgotten skill; they had only been practising with the guns for a few hours but it became apparent to me that under Richard and Martin's skilful instruction these raw recruits were becoming a very effective gun crew. They obviously did not have time to become as proficient as a full-time gunner of the past and they were not under naval discipline but they were certainly willing to learn. It was like watching a strange ritualistic dance because at first they did not have any powder or cannon balls. To see a gun crew miming the actions of loading and firing may have seemed amusing cannon to some eyes, but this was an essential part of their training. Cannon balls and powder were introduced when Richard and Martin were sure of their men's understanding of the task in hand, and they reorganised them several times to find which man was most suitable for each different task. All of this practice was essential to prevent accidents and injury from a recoiling gun. Each man had to be in the right place at the right time throughout the proceedings; there were minor accidents, but these were more probably to do with language difficulties caused by the understandably baffled interpreters, who also had to go through a learning curve. They were helped by being out in the sunshine and not on a dark lower deck of a heaving ship. I would love to have seen a complete battery of guns on an eighteenth-century warship at work after having witnessed the above with all the advantages bestowed upon these modern raw recruits.

above

HMS *Indefatigable* in a light swell in the tank at Yalta.

left

HMS *Indefatigable* in action with a Spanish frigate.

The Battle of Copenhagen, 1801, painted by Nicholas Pocock. Nelson famously put his telescope to his blind eye after a signal had been given to break off the action at this engagement. Various types of warships which were commonly in service at this time may be seen in this painting.
(National Maritime Museum, London)

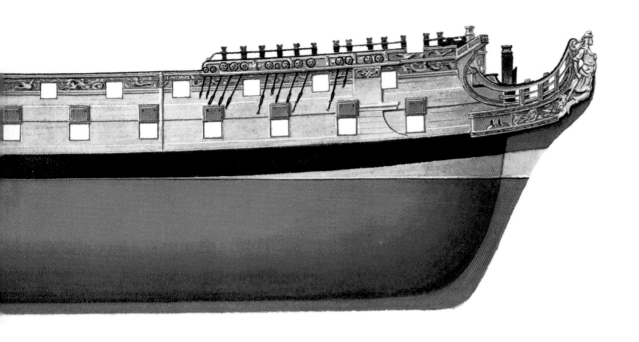

A profile view of a typical 74-gun third rate ship of the late eighteenth-century. This type of ship fought in most of the major fleet actions of the period. This one is HMS *Bellona*, based on the National Maritime Museum's coppering model, which probably depicts the ship after her Great Repair of 1778-1780.

(Painting by Ross Watton)

left

The models in a natural wind with their sails full. HMS *Indefatigable*, on the right, and the French frigate are being prepared to exchange gunfire. The crewman under HMS *Indefatigable*'s stern is attaching the rope to it (visible below the French frigate), which is used to control the models' movements during filming.

below

A general view of the pontoon set at Artek which was a full-sized set based upon the model of the 74-gun ship HMS *Justinian*. The interior of the lower decks can be seen to the right. On the far right is a section of upper gun deck which was used to support the rigging – which normally would be coming down from the missing upper masts and spars. This set was built on an old Russian Black Sea Fleet pontoon, part of which can be seen with the mooring ropes attached to the bollards (bottom right).

opposite page

A close-up of the figurehead on one of the 4-metre frigates. Some of the qualities of the styrofoam material used to fashion the figurehead can be seen with its rough finish. A 'dry brush' of paint (where very little paint is left on the brush head) has been dragged over the figurehead to give it a weathered appearance.

In a scene reminiscent of an eighteenth-century battle painting, several of the models engage in close action.

opposite page

HMS *Indefatigable* closes on the French frigate after setting fire to her with one last broadside. In this shot the frigate's mizzen mast was supposed to fall down but all that happened was the model's transom being badly damaged by the fire. The damage was later repaired at Pinewood. This picture was taken on the last day of filming the models in Yalta.

below

Two 4-metre frigates with some nearby wreckage floating on a choppy sea.

Three English frigates with HMS *Indefatigable* in the lead, firing her port side bow chaser. The wadding from the cannon can be seen on the right of the model with a smoke trail behind it. The model on the left is not actually in the tank but behind it – and it is only one metre high. It was made from wooden rods with sail material arranged to look like a man-of-war. To give this small model a bit of life during filming a man lay on his back with the model balanced on his feet and hands gently swaying it!

A figurehead on the *Grand Turk*. It was originally carved in polystyrene, then a mould was
taken and this was then laid up with resin and
fibreglass, giving this interesting result.

opposite page
HMS *Indefatigable* sails off into the mist in the
tank at Yalta.

A small English frigate catches the late afternoon breeze during a break in filming. The dark blue in the background is the sea. The lighter blue in the foreground is the water in the tank, ending at the line between the different blues. Most of the filming was done with the camera very close to the water to reduce the chances of producing the effect seen in this photograph.

3. Hornblower: An historical perspective

lthough Horatio Hornblower is a fictional character, C.S. Forester's inspiration for the books featuring his naval hero came from reports written by Royal Navy officers of the day, published in the *Naval Chronicle*. Forester found the reports to be dense in places, employing language and terminology alien to the twentieth century mind. He therefore cleverly rewrote them in his novels so that the reader could more readily identify with what was happening in the narrative. With the above in mind, I have chosen to include a very brief and broad outline of the major actions and events in which the Royal Navy was engaged in during the eighteenth century and early nineteenth century, to give the Hornblower ships and stories some historical context.

1759 20 November

Quiberon Bay. Admiral Sir Edward Hawke chased a French fleet of warships, in failing light, into the treacherous rock-strewn bay of Quiberon on the west coast of France. The French fleet, under the command of Admiral the Comte de Conflans, had escaped a blockade by the British in Brest, and was on its way to escort a fleet of transports intended for a planned invasion of Ireland. A significant part of the French fleet was either destroyed or rendered unfit for service; many of the ship's backs had broken as crews tried to extricate themselves from the two shallow rivers of the bay in which they had taken refuge during the action. British losses were remarkably light and the two ships which the Royal Navy lost were the result of being wrecked in stormy weather on the following day.

1768 25 August

Lieutenant James Cook (1728-79) left Plymouth in HMS *Endeavour* on his first voyage to search for the southern continent Terra Australis Incognita and to explore and chart the coast of New Zealand. In total Cook made three voyages of discovery in the Pacific Ocean, and for the first time accurately charted the east coast of Australia, New Zealand and other islands, aided by the newly developed chronometers (a very accurate clock) in his calculation of position and course. He also contributed towards the development of the healthy diet for his crews using 'sour kraut' (pickled cabbage), and the juice of oranges and lemons to prevent scurvy – a disease caused by the lack of vitamin C, which in the sixteenth and seventeenth centuries was responsible for great loss of life amongst ship's crews on voyages over six weeks in duration.

It was possible that in the happy-go-lucky Spanish navy the officer of the watch over there did not know that no sloop like Le Reve was attached to the fleet – or even possibly by a miracle there might be one. Le Reve was French built and French rigged, after all. Side by side Le Reve and the battleship sailed over the lumpy sea. They were within point-blank range of fifty big guns, when one well-aimed shot would sink them.

Mr. Mishipman Hornblower

1775-83

War of American Independence. Declaration of American Independence 4 July 1776.

1779 14 February

Murder of Cook (by this time promoted to his better known rank of Captain) on the Sandwich Islands (later Hawaii).

1780 16 January

Battle of St Vincent – sometimes referred to as the 'Moonlight Battle'. Admiral Sir George Rodney (1719-92) was escorting a large convoy of much needed supplies for Gibraltar and Minorca when a Spanish fleet of eleven ships of the line and two frigates were sighted, under the command of Admiral Don Juan de Langara, in the vicinity of Cape St Vincent (now in southern Portugal). In deteriorating weather, Rodney pursued the Spanish fleet and after an all-night action only four ships of the line and two frigates of the original Spanish fleet were still afloat.

1782 12 April

Battle of the Saints. The 'Saints' were a group of small islets in the West Indies, between Guadeloupe and Dominica. A British fleet under the command of Admiral Sir George Rodney, with thirty-six ships of the line, fought an action against a French fleet of thirty ships under the command of Vice Admiral the Comte de Grasse, who was escorting a French convoy. During the action de Grasse was taken prisoner. This action is mainly remembered for the introduction of the tactic of breaking the line, but also marked the final sea-battle of the American War of Independence.

1782 22 August

The 100-gun ship HMS *Royal George* sank at Spithead off Portsmouth with the loss of 900 lives including Admiral Richard Kempenfelt, who was flying his flag on board. The accident occurred while the ship was heeled over to enable repairs to be carried out to her bottom. There are two schools of thought as to why she sank. The first is that water entered through her lower gun ports while she was heeled too far over; the other possible explanation is that rotten timbers caused part of her bottom to fall out.

1783 3 September

End of War of American Independence with the Treaty of Versailles between Britain, France, Spain and America.

1789 28 April

Fletcher Christian led a successful mutiny against Captain Bligh on board the armed transport HMS *Bounty*; the ship was on a mission to collect breadfruit seedlings from Tahiti.

1794 1 June

Battle of Ushant – also known as Battle of the Glorious First of June. A fleet under the command of Admiral Howe (1726-99) was waiting in the eastern Atlantic for a French grain convoy; this convoy was escorted by a fleet of warships under the command of Admiral Villaret-Joyeuse. After a desperate melee many French ships were damaged or captured, but the grain convoy made it home – saving the French admiral from the guillotine.

1797 February

Battle of Cape St Vincent. A Fleet of fifteen ships of the line under the command of Admiral Sir John Jervis (1735-1823) were lying in wait for the Spanish fleet. During the ensuing engagement the British captured four Spanish ships of the line out of an original fleet of twenty-seven, under the command of Admiral don Jose de Cordova off the Portuguese coast. Cordova was bound for Brest to join the combined fleets of France and Holland, to assist them in gaining control of the English Channel for a planned invasion of Britain. Commodore Horatio Nelson (1758-1805) distinguished himself by capturing the 112-gun *San Josef* and 80-gun *San Nicolas*. The Spanish fleet was left heavily damaged and in a state of disarray after the British victory, although Jervis was later criticised for not pursuing the defeated fleet after the battle. Jervis was made Earl St. Vincent and Nelson was also rewarded with a knighthood for his part in this action.

1797 16 April

The ships of the Channel fleet mutinied at Spithead against pay and conditions in naval service. However, since it was felt that the men were justified in their actions no one was court marshalled and the men actually did receive an increase in pay. This was followed by a mutiny at the Nore led by Richard Parker, which ended with the hanging from the yard arm of Parker and twenty-four seamen after a court marshal.

1798 1 and 2 August

The Battle of the Nile – also known as the Battle of Aboukir Bay. The Royal Navy under Nelson's command destroyed the French fleet, which was anchored in a defensive line across the bay under Admiral Francois Brueys. The supply fleet, down the coast at Alexandria, was still intact and had to be dealt with later.

1805 21 October

The battle of Trafalgar. Some weeks before the battle, Admiral Lord Nelson had pursued the French admiral, the Comte de Villeneneuve, across the Atlantic to the West Indies and back. Villeneuve was trying to decoy Nelson away from Europe as part of Napoleon's preparations for yet another proposed invasion of Britain. This strategy failed, and Villeneuve returned to Cadiz. Villeneuve left Cadiz in the company of the Spanish Fleet under the command of Admiral Gravina; they were confident of a victory over the smaller British fleet. The French fleet formed a loose line off the Cape of Trafalgar which Nelson cut through in two places, leading with HMS *Victory* and followed by Admiral Collingwood in HMS *Royal Sovereign*. After a savage action, the ships of the combined French and Spanish fleets were all either captured or put to flight. The loss of life during the action, and during the storm which followed was measured in thousands. Most significantly for the Royal Navy, Nelson was lost to a musket ball fired from the top of a French ship, the *Redoutable*.

4. Hornblower's Ship Types

The eighteenth century saw many developments in the production and variety of the sailing warship. Fleets contained ships of varying size and armament; although these ships had several responsibilities, none were taken more seriously than their role in battle. One distinguishing characteristic was the number of guns aboard a given vessel. This feature soon became a frame of reference and ships were recognised by their number of guns – 74-gun, 64-gun, and so on. The late 1800s saw lighter armaments incorporated onto larger vessels and so this classification was not always entirely accurate.

Ships which carried over 20 guns were given a rating. Vessels were rated from one to six and the ships were awarded their ratings essentially in terms of their size. 100-gun ships such as HMS *Victory* were classed as first rate, whilst small frigates would receive a fifth or sixth rating. A ship's rating would also disclose information about the size of the crew, and affect their wages and the number of officers onboard (all increased with ship's rating).

The demand for warships and trading ships was growing during the eighteenth century and the Royal Navy had many bases and anchorage's around the coasts of Britain; these were mainly along the south coast within easy reach of its main adversaries, France, Holland and Spain. The main ones – Portsmouth, Plymouth and the various dockyards along the upper and lower reaches of the Thames – serviced and built the various warships required by the navy. There were many smaller yards which built famous warships and one which still survives at Bucklers Hard, on the Beaulieu river in the New Forest in southern England, built Nelson's favourite ship HMS *Agamemnon* in 1781.

The main construction material used was oak timber although later in the period, when suitable oak was in short supply, some ships (especially frigates) were built from fir. The quantities of timber required to build a ship were enormous as the following example shows.

The 74-gun ship HMS *Triumph* consumed 3028 loads, (a load was 50 cubic feet of timber, equivalent to a substantial tree) of which 1355 were of compass oak (used for making all the curved parts). Another 597 were of straight oak for the sternpost and other parts and 62 loads of elm were used in the keel. One hundred and thirty five loads of fir were consumed for sundry purposes, along with 61 loads for square knees and 76 loads for raking knees. (Lavery 1991: 62)

This timber had to be transported without modern facilities such as lorries and mechanised cranes, but with sweat of men and horses (although some goods were also brought by water). Timber had to be stored while it seasoned which meant the dockyards had to have large areas devoted to its storage.

The Loire was going faster through the water than Hotspur, gaining in the race to that extent. Everyone knew that French ship designers were cleverer than English ones; French ships were usually faster.

Hornblower and the 'Hotspur'

The Nelson era was the dawn of the industrial age. Steam power was in its infancy and was not yet being used widely in industrial processes. Ships were built by apprenticeship-served shipwrights, and everything was labour-intensive. The first production stage required the supply of suitable wood; sawyers working in pairs over saw pits were to start converting the tree trunks into the useable sizes and shapes required to build the ships. Shipwrights using hand tools, the principle ones being the adze and axe, finished the shaping of the component parts. The parts were held together by nails, bolts and trenails hammered into holes bored with large hand-driven augers (a type of drill). Other trades used in the construction of wooden ships included the caulkers who hammered oakum into the gaps between the ship's planks before it was tarred to make it water tight; blacksmiths made the iron knees, which were being introduced to replace the wooden ones together with the chains used on the channels and various other parts employed on the ship's hull, masts and spars; foundries cast the cannons and balls, and on the lower reaches of the river Thames there were powder mills which manufactured the gun powder to fire the various types of armament. Sails lofts had sailmakers producing the sails and ropewalks for the spinning of the miles and miles of different types of cordage required in the rigging of a ship.

On top of the work which the yards did in building the ships, there were a number of additional duties – most importantly maintenance. A wooden ship, by its very nature, is very labour intensive and to keep a vessel in good working order requires a programme of constant care whilst in service to prevent premature failure of its many parts. The replacement of worn and rotten timbers caused by movement and bad ventilation below decks, especially in the underwater areas like the orlop deck and stowage above the keel, was essential. Another important job, which had to be done at regular intervals, was the scraping of ships' bottoms to remove the build up of marine growth, which had the effect of slowing a ship's progress through the water. Any defective planks below the water-line would also be replaced while the ship was out of the water. To this end most dockyards had either slips or dry docks to work on the underwater parts. In 1761, the navy experimented with nailing copper plates to the bottom of the frigate HMS *Alarm* to reduce the problem of marine growth and to prevent the ravages in warmer waters of the feared Teredo Worm, which in previous times had been responsible for the bottoms of ships literally dropping out because the pests had bored so many holes in the timbers that the structure fell apart, sometimes with disastrous consequences. Copper plates fixed with iron nails were very successful at first, until it was discovered that galvanic action between the iron fixings and the copper plates caused the plates to drop off prematurely. This problem was later solved by the introduction of copper fixing bolts. Once the problems of galvanic action had been overcome, the use of copper as an anti-fouling on ships' bottoms became general practice in navies world-wide. This meant that ships

A bow view of HMS *Justinian* after she had finished her work in the tank. She is being disassembled ready to go into storage.

could now safely venture into warm waters without the constant fear of rot caused by worm action and they could spend as much as six months at sea – a very useful attribute when on blockade duty off the ports of western France and Spain. The copper still needed regular cleaning and repair but it was a major contribution to the safety of the ships' structure allowing longer voyages at sea to be undertaken.

The 74-gun Ship HMS Justinian

The largest type of ship featured in the Hornblower series was the third rate, 74-gun ship HMS *Justinian*, from a class evolved by the French in the 1740s. The British adopted the type as a standard ship-of-the-line in 1755 and it was to become the most common type of ship to be found in the Royal Navy, making up about half of the Navy List through to the nineteenth century. Most of the major fleet actions in the late eighteenth and early nineteenth centuries mostly involved 74-gun ships on both sides. The 74 had at least two features which contributed towards its success. Firstly, it was a relatively fast ship when compared to a more heavily armed first rate, and according to some estimates was as fast as a frigate. Secondly, it was capable of carrying a battery of 32-pounder cannons on its lower gun deck, heavy enough to be used in major fleet actions. Some of the first and second rates, especially in the French and Spanish navies, used a 42-pound gun on their lower deck, but the British favoured the 32-pounder; the British gun which had a good penetrating power combined with a rapid rate of fire. It was found that using a 42-pound ball was just beyond the limits of human muscle power to load rapidly when in action. Sixteen 74s were in action at the Battle of Trafalgar in Nelson's fleet, from a total of 27 ships-of-the-line (excluding the four frigates and two smaller craft also present). Sir Thomas Slade, who was surveyor to the navy from 1755-71, conceived the Common Class of 74 which carried 18-pounders on its upper deck with fourteen or fifteen ports per side, based upon an older French design with fifteen ports per side. Bately, Williams and Rule all designed 74s but they were not as successful as the original Slade design, which continued in use many years beyond his death.

HMS *Justinian*, which features in the first episode of Hornblower, was based upon the French 74 *Le Superbe* of 1785. The drawings were obtained by Andrew Mollo (production designer) from the Musée de la Marine in Paris. These drawings were the basis for the model and the pontoon set used in the production. Of all the models this was the most complete, featuring many deck details not found on any of the other models. It took the longest time to build, approximately three months, and was a source of great frustration to me. The original order stated that it was to be 10 metres (32 feet) long and was to be built for the very reasonable price of $35,000. The start of the model's construction was delayed by many weeks as a result of a management change in the production company, who were slow in confirming the order. This was the most complex model and it needed a great deal of interpretative work from the drawings, more than any of the others. The delay in confirming the order had a beneficial effect because, while the yard was waiting for the confirmation to start building, they were gaining much needed experience on the other models. When the order was finally confirmed, a compromise was reached and the length of the HMS *Justinian* model was reduced to 5 metres (15 feet).

On approaching the model of HMS *Justinian* in the water, the first thing that you notice is its size, which gives it a presence unequalled among the other models. The hull is much taller with its two rows of gun ports and the masts and spars are of a more substantial proportion. All of the decks have planking except the well (or weather) deck below the boat tier. The forecastle and quarter deck guns are complete with tackles at their ports. Access to the interior of the hull is through a removable hatch in the well deck. The gunports are all designed to open and each one has its own dummy cannon on a simplified carriage. The carriages are held in position by velcro tape, allowing working ones to be exchanged in their place. Unfortunately none of the episodes had a need for HMS *Justinian* to fire her cannons in anger. The loading of all of the cannons would indeed have been an interesting exercise. The interior of the hull had been designed to allow easy access to all of the gunports from inside; this was done by putting the guns on two shelves fixed just below the ports on both sides. A walkway (or more aptly, crawlway) ran from bow to stern; this allowed, with some considerable neck craning, a view of the outside world through the stern galleries. The interior was very roomy before the model was put into the water, but once the ballast had been put aboard there was not a lot of room left. This model is first seen in the opening scenes of the first episode at Spithead and is the first ship that the young Hornblower serves on. In this guise it is shown as an English 74 with the characteristic ochre and black stripes along the outside of the hull, later standardised in the time of Nelson. When the team were discussing how the viewing public were to differentiate the various ships from France, England and Spain it was decided to give them a different colour scheme for each country to make identification easier. English ships were to have black and ochre bands, French ships natural wood with a red band and the Spanish were to be black and yellow against natural wood. The HMS *Justinian* model played other roles as a Spanish and an English ship. It was initially painted to be an English ship which meant that all of the natural wood was already painted when it came to be repainted as a Spanish ship; according to the colour scheme above, this meant that she looked French, but as the Spanish were allies of the French it saved having to scrape the paint off in the middle of an already pressing schedule.

As a reference for the colour schemes, I used HMS *Victory* as a starting point. Other features were included from the 74-gun HMS *Bellona* launched in 1760, which is too early for the Hornblower period but proved useful for some of the details on the stern galleries. The main body of the hull was painted in ochre and black bands; the black on the outside of the gunport doors giving, when the doors are closed, a distinctive checkerboard effect. The inside of the doors were painted a dark red ochre, as were all of the visible internal areas of the ship. The decorative stern was initially painted yellow ochre and the dark blue background surrounding the relief work was painted afterwards. The bright red area above the open gallery was treated in the same way. Finally, the off-white tracery on the win-

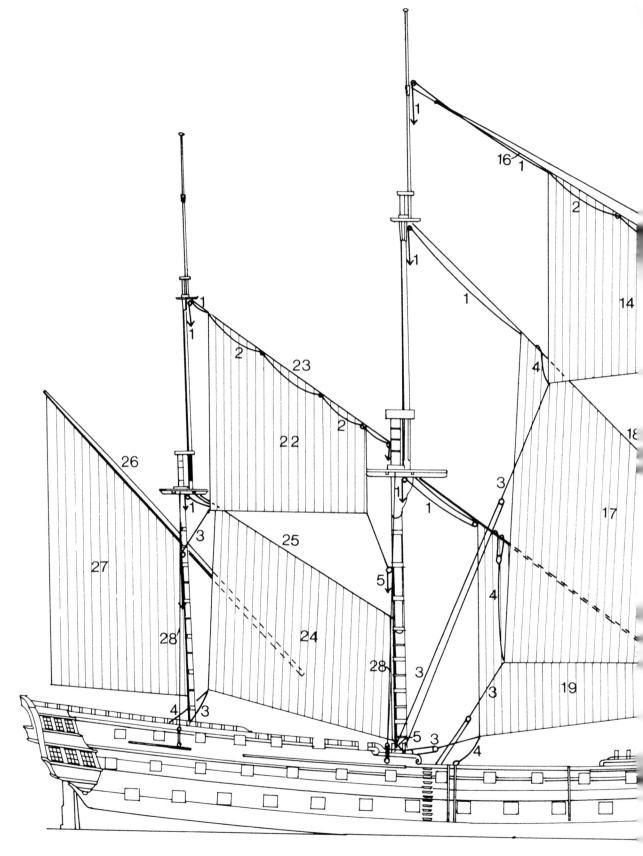

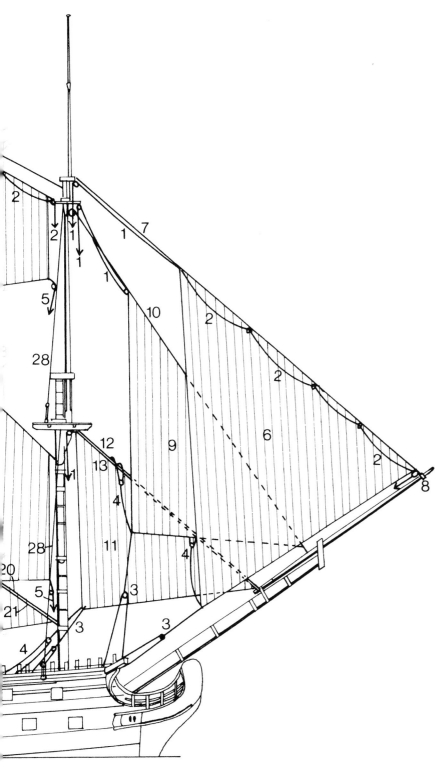

Plan showing the fore and aft sails of a 74-gun ship, HMS *Bellona*, before her middle staysail was added in 1773. HMS *Justinian* and other ships of her class would have been fitted similarly. No scale.

1. Halyards
2. Downhaulers
3. Sheets
4. Lee sheets
5. Tacks
6. Jibsail
7. Jibsail stay
8. Jib traveller
9. Fore topsail
10. Fore topsail stay
11. Fore staysail
12. Fore stay
13. Fore staysail stay
16. Main topgallant staysail stay
17. Main top staysail
18. Main top preventer stay
19. Main staysail
20. Main stay
21. Main staysail stay
22. Mizzen tops staysail
23. Main topmast stay
24. Mizzen staysail
25. Mizzen staysail stay
26. Mizzen yard
27. Mizzen course
28. Shrouds used to secure blocks affecting staysail rigging

(Source: Lavery, 1985)

Longitudinal section of a 74-gun ship, HMS *Bellona*, showing the features that would have been present on board many ships of her rating – such as HMS *Justinian*. 1/192 scale.

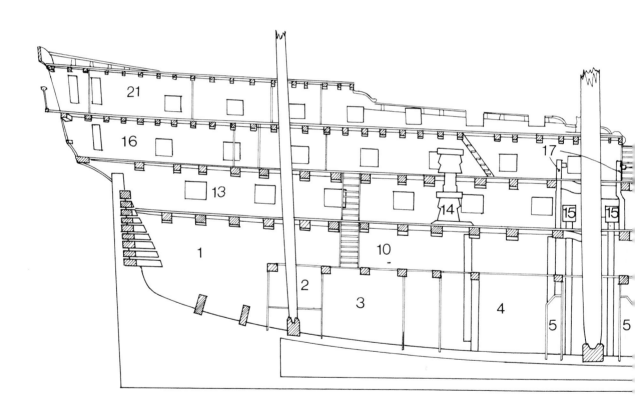

1. Bread room
2. Powder room
3. Spirit room
4. After hold
5. Shot lockers
6. Main hold
7. Main magazine
8. Filling room

9. Light room
10. After cockpit
11. Sail rooms
12. Carpenter's, gunner's and
    boatswain's store rooms
13. Gun room
14. Main capstan
15. Pumps

16. Wardroom
17. Jeer bitts
18. Fore jeer capstan
19. Fire hearth
20. Jeer bitts
21. Captain's cabin
(Source: Lavery, 1985)

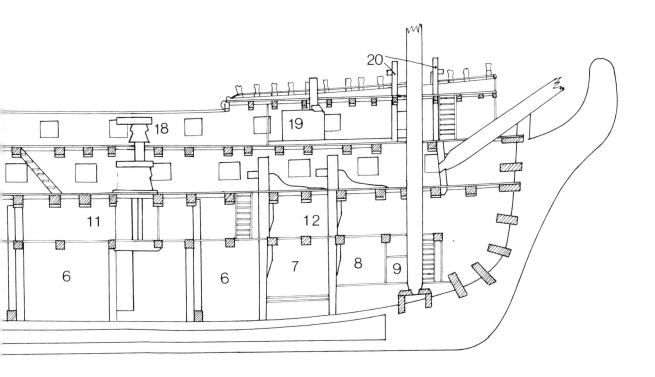

dows was painted in. The deck guns were given yellow ochre carriages with black gun barrels, trucks and wheels. I have often found that using black straight from the can gives a very stark look to models and they appear very unrealistic, so all of the colours were softened (in the case of black with white and brown). I felt that the underwater part of the hull, whilst not being visible except at the water-line, needed to be as realistic as possible. To this end, and to imitate the coppered bottom, it was painted dark green (imitating the verdigris colour of copper exposed to the air).

On an English ship it was common practice in a number of classes of warship to have the belfry at the break of the focastle. The reason that I have brought your attention to this detail is because the pontoon set features the belfry several times in the background of many scenes and I felt anyone who is familiar with English warships from this period would be puzzled as to why it was there. The supporting legs of the belfry were painted yellow ochre and the roof black on both the model and the pontoon set. The bell on the full-sized set was a real brass one, but the model had a turned wooden one painted a brass colour. To my mind the belfry on HMS *Justinian* is in the wrong place at the break of the poop deck for an English ship. A common practice in the Royal Navy was, after having captured ships from the French or Spanish, they were refitted and then used against their old masters, sometimes using their old name or given a new one. HMS *Justinian*, although it is not part of any of the Hornblower plots, falls into this category.

Profile of a 74-gun ship: HMS *Bellona*

The 74-gun ship formed the backbone of the Royal Navy and her opponents in the Napoleonic Wars. Between 1755-1815 more than 200 of these ships served with the Royal Navy alone

Date entered into service	1760
Rating	Third
Length of gun deck	168ft
Depth of hold	19ft 9in
Breadth of beam	46ft 9in
Tonnage	1615 tons
Number of guns	1812: twenty-eight 32pdrs; twenty-eight 28pdrs; eight 12pdrs; ten 32pdr carronades; two 18pdr carronades; two 12pdr carronades
Crew complement	1760: 650 men 1805: 590 men
Cost of building	£43,391

(Source: Lavery 1985)

The 'Razee' HMS Indefatigable

This is how I last saw the *Grand Turk* – from the deck of a yacht at the Portsmouth Festival of Sea. The most notable change in her appearance is more appropriate figurehead which is more in keeping with her name.

Captain Edward Pellew, who featured in the early episodes of Hornblower, was a real character and the ship HMS *Indefatigable* is likewise based upon his ship of the same name captained by Pellew. Ordered on 3 August 1780 from Bucklers Hard in the New Forest as a 64-gun, two-decker Ardent class, (designed by Slade, who also designed HMS *Victory*), launched in July 1784 as a sister to Nelson's HMS *Agamemnon*. In 1795 the 64-gun ship was no longer deemed suitable as a ship-of-the-line, so HMS *Indefatigable* along with HMS *Anson* and HMS *Magnanime*, was 'razeed', a process whereby the upper deck was cut down to make a single-decked fifth rate, with a nominal rating of 44 guns, in response to the development of French warships of the same class carrying more and heavier guns. These cut down ships proved to be fairly successful as a intermediate measure until the Royal Navy could construct purpose-built frigates to combat the new class of French heavy frigates. HMS *Indefatigable* kept the sail plan from the bigger 64-gun ship and

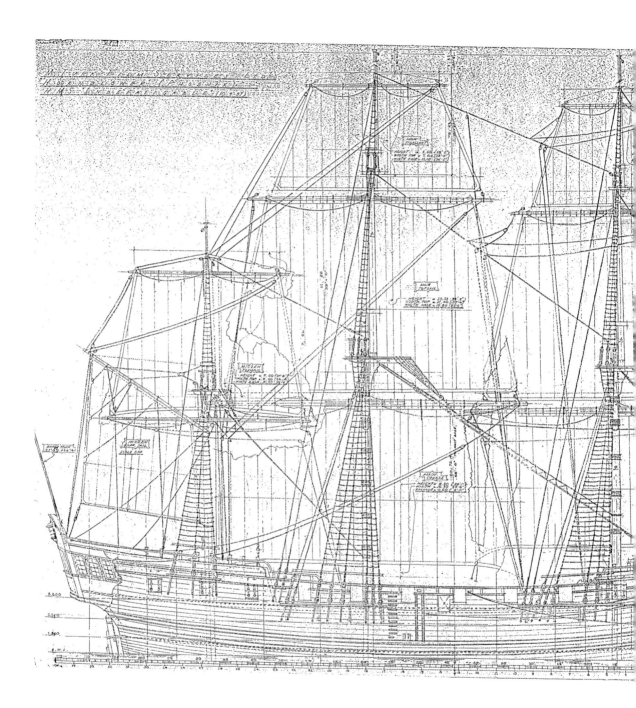

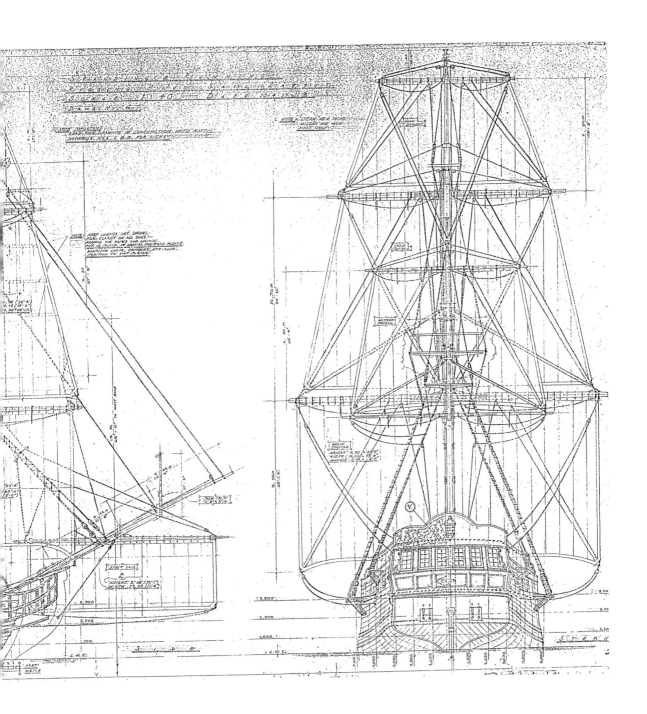

Grand Turk. Designed by John Heath and owned by Mike Turk, I originally knew this model as the *Phoenix*, hence the name on the drawings. The ship played HMS *Indefatigable* and the French frigate *Papillon*. Scale as shown. (Source: author)

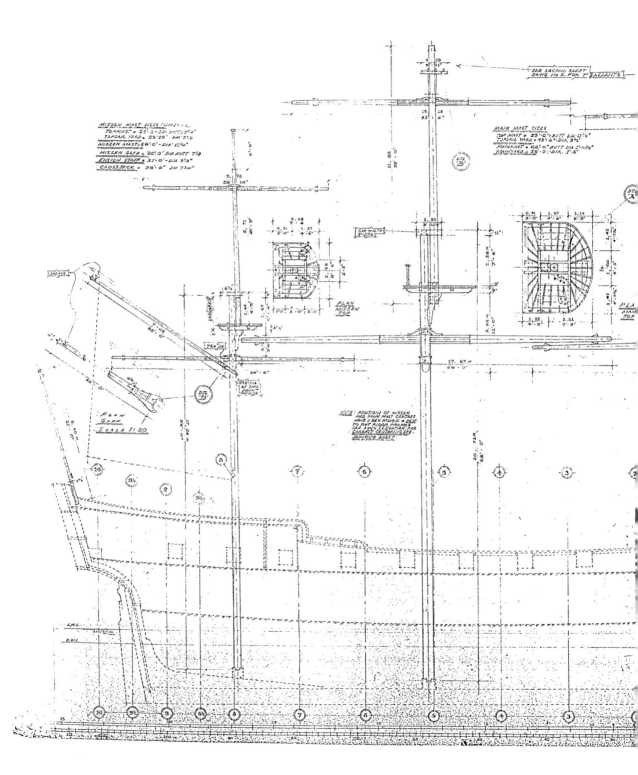

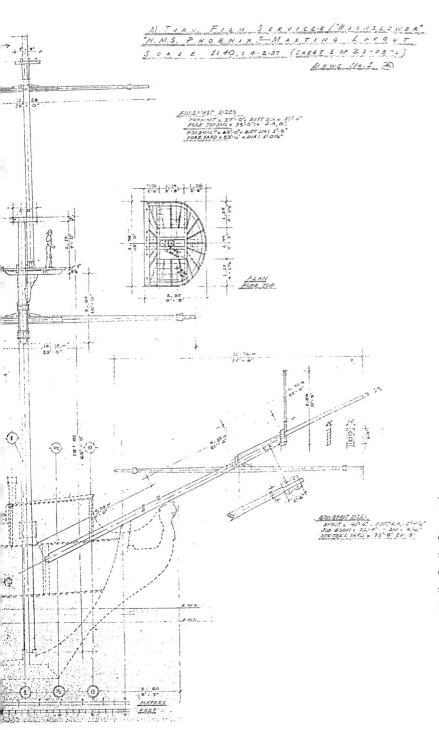

The masts, yards and tops of *Grand Turk*, showing the detail that was so often hidden by the sails when the models were in use. Scale as shown on rule at bottom (not at the ratio shown).
(Source: author)

Another plan of *Grand Turk*, which can be compared to the artist's impression of HMS *Blandford* (pages 104-5), which was one of the historical ships that the 'razeed' HMS *Indefatigable* (played by *Grand Turk*) was based upon for the series. Scale as shown.

(Source: author)

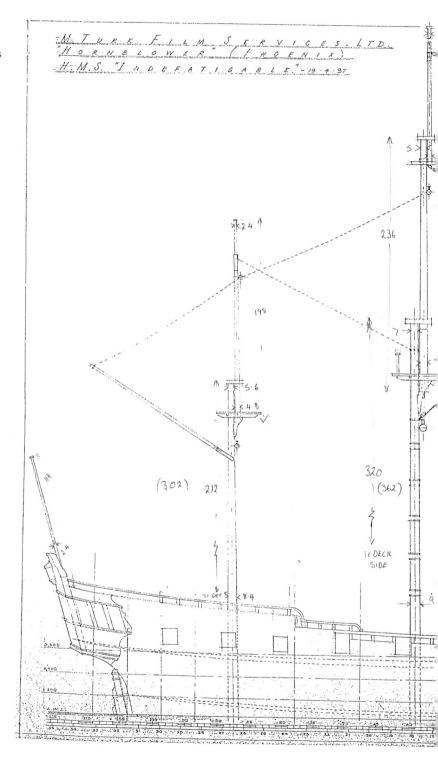

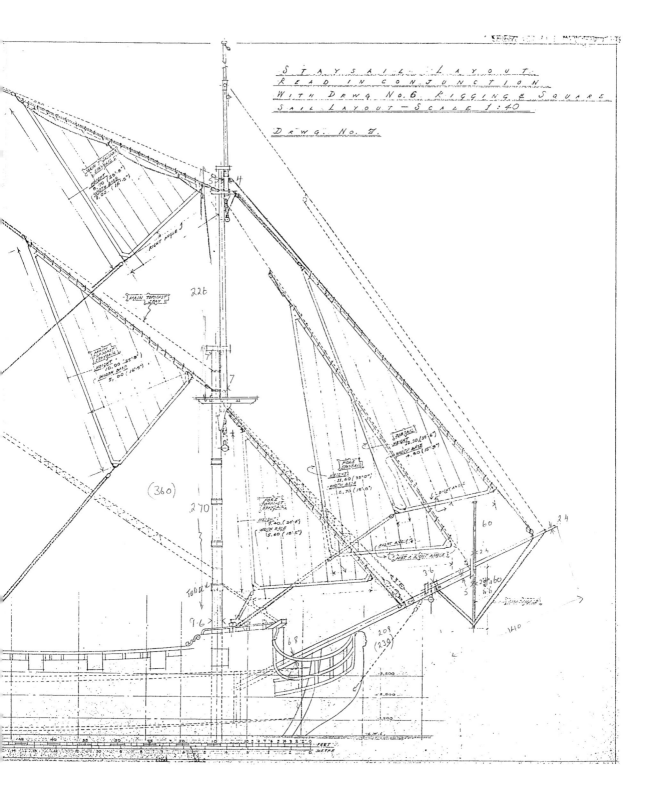

STAYSAIL LAYOUT
READ IN CONJUNCTION
WITH DRWG No.6 RIGGING & SQUARE
SAIL LAYOUT — SCALE 1:40

DRWG. No. 7.

a gun battery consisting of 42-pounder carronades and 24-pounder long guns. The carronade at this time was a relatively recent development and they were not included in a ship's rating. This combination gave her a very useful turn of speed with a broadside weight capable of meeting the new French heavy frigates on more than equal terms.

The Hornblower full-sized replica version of HMS *Indefatigable* started life as the *Phoenix* being built at Marmaris in Turkey on the Black Sea coast. It had been commissioned as a twelfth-century merchant ship for an Arnold Schwarzenegger film

Grand Turk at her mooring in Artek harbour. She arrived from Turkey, where she was built but not completed. The rigging is being completed and no sails have been put on yet. In the background is Bear Rock which featured several times in the background of the first two Hornblower episodes

that was never made. Andrew Mollo tracked down the ship in Marmaris and found that it consisted of a keel and a few frames. A deal was struck between Mike Turk, the ship's owner, and the Hornblower company for the completion of the ship. They used HMS *Blandford*, a 20-gun sixth rate launched on 13 February 1720, as the basis for HMS *Indefatigable's* external features. The hull and internal structures were designed by John Heath and he was assisted by Ian McDougal. I gather from talking to John Heath that building the *Grand Turk*, as the completed ship is now known, was an interesting experience for someone who is more used to working with modern sea craft. The main structures of the ship are built from Iroko; the frames were individually made up in laminations as opposed to using the traditional method of built-up frames from compass timber joined together in sections. Externally the ship looks as though she belongs to the eighteenth century, but internally she is very modern with many safety features, as you would expect to find in such a recently fitted ship. The *Grand Turk* has comfortable headroom and there is a well-equipped galley and crew accommodation. Two 450-horsepower Kelvin diesel motors, down on the equivalent of the orlop deck, provide enough power to make the ship independent of wind power. Additionally there are bow thrusters for manoeuvring in enclosed spaces. The *Grand Turk* weighs 314 tons and the hull is 36 metres (119 feet) long and 10 metres (34 feet) wide. Above the water the foremast is 35 metres (117 feet), the main 35 metres (117 feet) and the mizzen 27 metres (90 feet). In the films she is shown with period anchors but these are just dressing – she is equipped with modern anchors and winches to handle them. The capstan seen on the films is a mock up and has no function at all. The standing rigging is steel cable with modern synthetic rope for the running rigging. The wheel on the poop deck, although it works, is not necessary to steer the ship – beside the wheel is a replica eighteenth-century binnacle which hides a computer-controlled steering and navigation system. The ten cannons positioned on the well deck are the only ones fitted, although the ship has ten gunports a side.

Profile of a 20-gun ship: HMS *Blandford*

Along with 24-gun ships, the 20-gun ship was the smallest class regularly commanded by a Post Captain. The design origin of this type of ship appears to date back to the mid-seventeenth century.

Date entered into service	1720
Rating	Sixth
Length of gun deck	106ft
Depth of hold	9ft 2in
Breadth of beam	28ft 6in
Tonnage	364 tons
Number of guns	Twenty 6pdrs
Crew complement	120-130 men
Cost of building	£3521

(Source: Goodwin 1988)

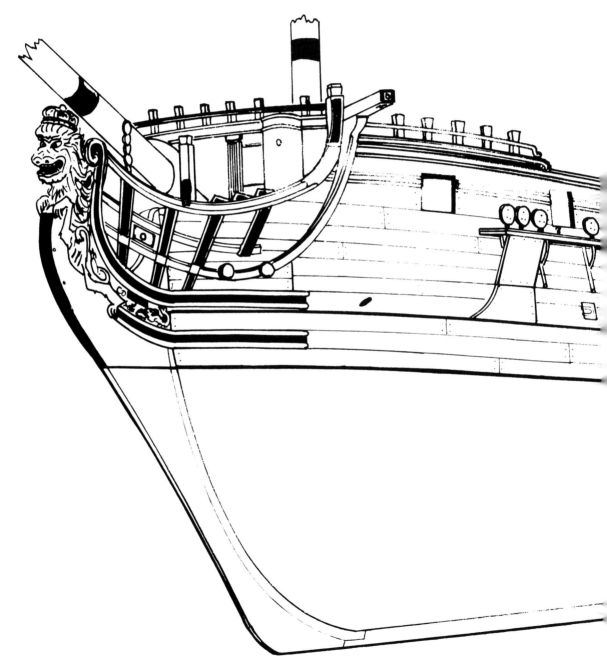

A view of HMS *Blandford*'s hull, based on the Science Museum model.
HMS *Blandford* was a 20-gun ship in the Royal Navy, and was useful as a guide
for making the full-sized *Grand Turk* appear as the 'razeed' HMS *Indefatigable* in
the series. This drawing is an interesting comparison to the models shown in
this book's photographs. No scale.
(Source: Goodwin, 1988)

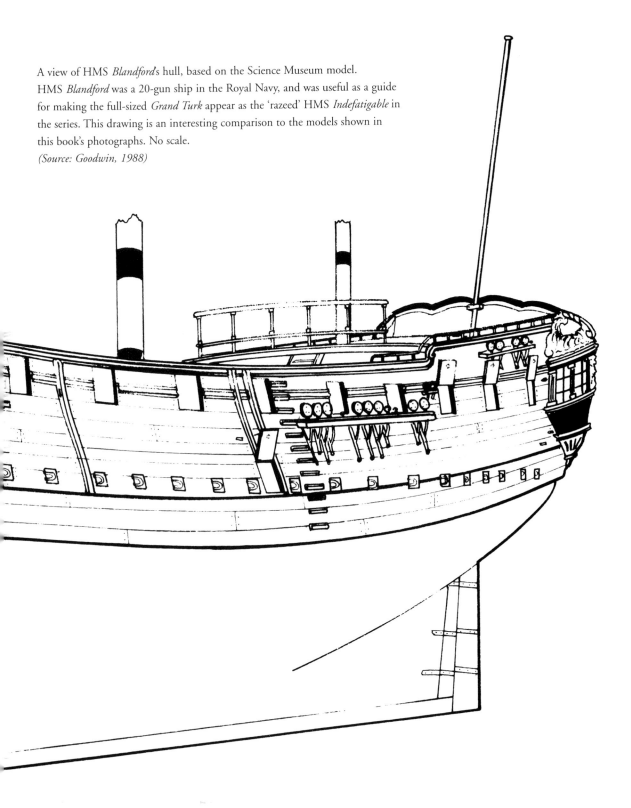

A plan of HMS *Blandford*'s upper deck. The 20-gun HMS *Blandford* was used as the basis for HMS *Indefatigable*'s external features. 1/96 scale.

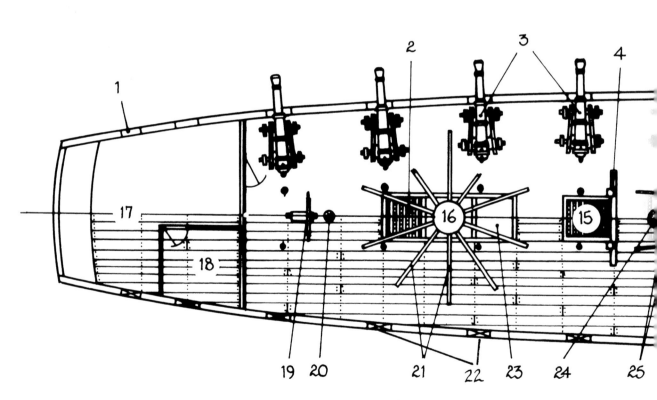

1. Quarter light
2. Ventilation grating
3. 6pdr cannon
4. Main jeer bitts
5. Cannon in run in position
6. Ventilation grating
7. Galley ventilation flue
8. Fore topsail sheet bitts
9. Bowsprit
10. Fore mast
11. Fore access hatchway
12. Fore hatch
13. Access hatchway
14. Main hatch
15. After hatch
16. Capstan
17. Captain's day cabin
18. Captain's sleeping berth
19. Steering wheel
20. Mizzen mast
21. Capstan bars (partially omitted for clarity)
22. Gunports
23. After access hatchway
24. Main mast
25. Elm tree pumps
26. Main topsail sheet bitts
27. Ringbolts for the training tackle
28. Galley firehearth flue
29. Fore jeer bitts
30. Forecastle bulkhead
31. Roundhouse

(Source: Goodwin, 1988)

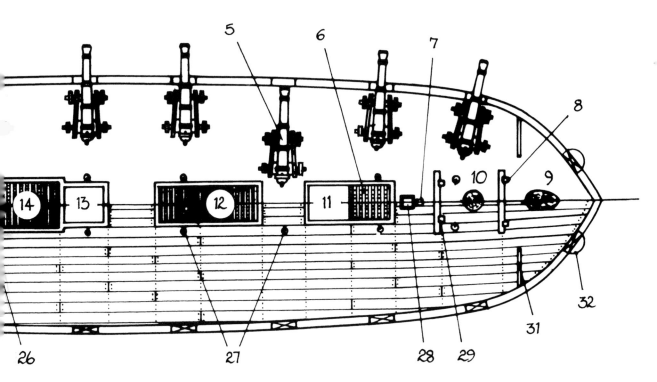

The Ukrainian crew are busy preparing the English and Spanish 4-metre frigates for launching. The masts have been stepped and the standing rigging is mostly in place. The sails are furled and the running rigging is hanging in little balls from them. The crude, unsafe ladder used to work on the model's rigging can just be seen behind the model on the right.

The Frigates

The frigate was the most sought after type of ship to serve on by naval officers and crew for several reasons. They tended to be more independent of the fleets with their demanding admirals, who frequently complained that they did not have enough frigates. The frigate crews had more chance of a larger proportion of any prize as their independence meant that there was not usually another ship in sight with which prize money would have been shared. Frigates were faster in a given wind condition than ships larger than themselves, so they could also stay out of trouble and they were generally more comfortable to live in because the crew did not have to share their living space with the ship's cannons; they lived below the gun deck in a separate deck space. This extra space afforded by the lack of guns on the accommodation deck allowed them to have personal sea chests for their possessions, and it was most probably warmer without gun ports, which would let in drafts.

Frigates underwent a considerable development throughout the eighteenth century. The first 'true' frigates were armed with nine- to twelve-pounder cannons in the main battery. By the time the century was drawing to a close they had greatly increased in size, number of cannon and weight of broadside, carrying as many as forty-four cannon and firing ball from eighteen to twenty-four pounds in weight. They were useful for fighting in relatively bad weather because their main gun deck was higher above the waterline, thus reducing the chance of the sea coming through an open gunport which was a common problem on a number of ship types at the time.

Three 4-metre (13 feet) long frigate type ships were built for the Hornblower production. They all started with lines taken from Chapman's *Archiectura Navalis Mercatoria* (1768) and David Steel's *Naval Architecture*. The lines were then redrawn by Pavel Martuikov into an approximation of a merchant ship, frigate and corvette. The closest drawing to the finished models are those of the *Three Sisters* from Steel's drafts but they are not definitive – model makers should not look to these references hoping to build a replica of one of the frigates because enormous liberties were taken with the original drawings. With these lines as a starting point, we sat in an office and used our knowledge and imaginations to create generalised Spanish, French and English ship's of the period. At various points in the Hornblower series these models play many different roles including a merchantman, a corvette, as well as frigates of all three nationalities. They are sometimes all seen together in harbour scenes, and one of them has been blown up at least twice to my knowledge. The English frigate has even been seen playing a French ship on more than one occasion. This is the nature of the film industry – liberties have to be taken with historical fact due to the demands of a schedule.

These frigate models were not of total fantasy. All of the deck arrangements and external features were based upon Chapman and Steel's drawings and many other reference books listed in the bibliography were used. There is, however, not enough space in this book for me to list where each individual part for the models came from. The team tried to stay within the spirit of each nationalities' ships; for example the forward shroud on the French ship was given blocks instead of deadeyes and the angle on the sternpost was made more vertical than on an English ship. The Spanish frigate was given an offset jib boom with a more flamboyant stern decoration. Seen from a distance it is very difficult to tell them apart; it is only when you get closer that these subtle differences become apparent. The rigging plan for all three came directly from Chapman's rigging plan for a frigate. They were all built below the waterline using the diagonal planking system sometimes called cold moulding. Above the waterline they were strip planked. Three figureheads were carved – a lion rampant, a unicorn and a young woman – and each figurehead was interchangeable and could be fitted to any one of the models. Individual sails could be used on any of the models and although the spars were

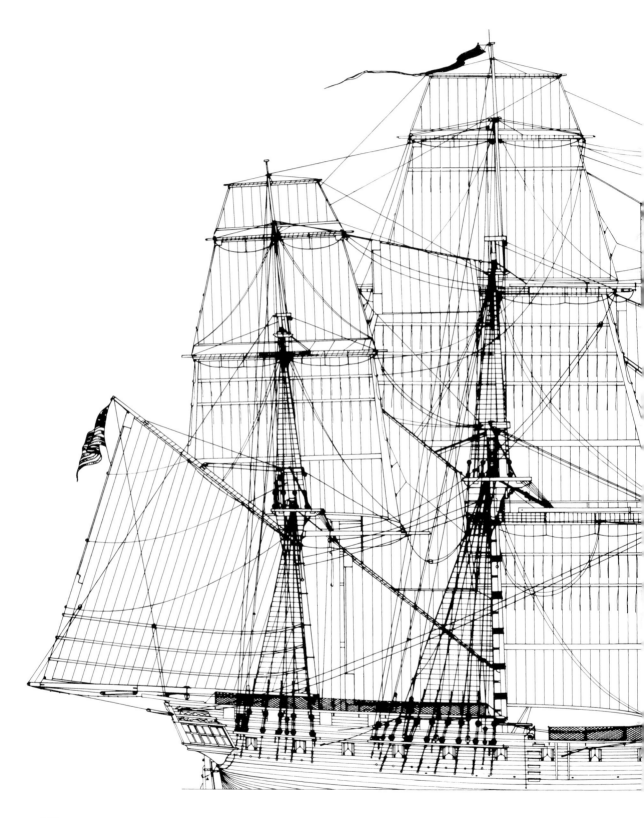

Complete sail plan of *Essex*, an American frigate. Although frigates were smaller ships than 74-gun third raters, their sail plans were no less complicated, and this was not ignored on the models which we built. No scale.
(Source: Takajian, 1990)

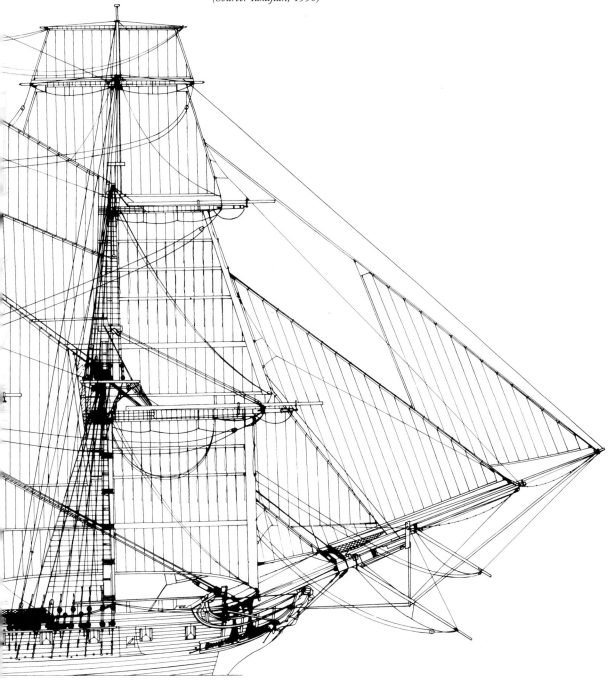

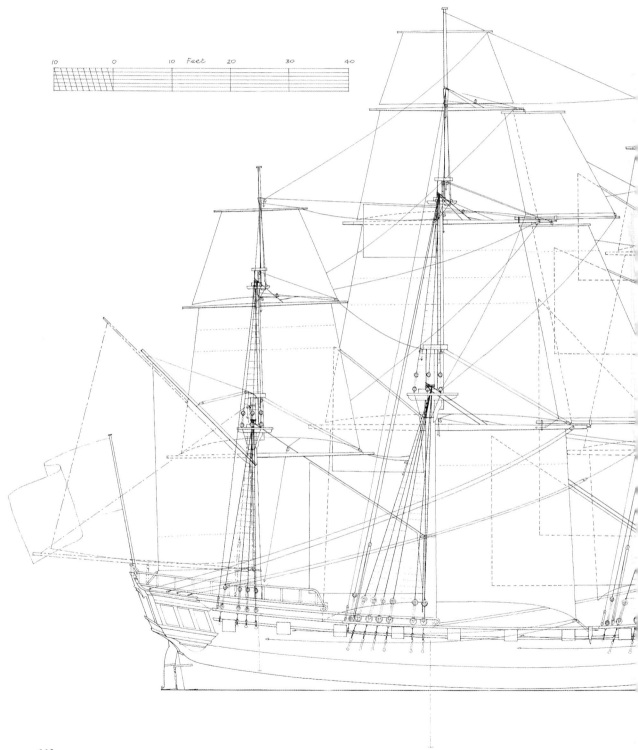

10   0   10 Feet 20   30   40

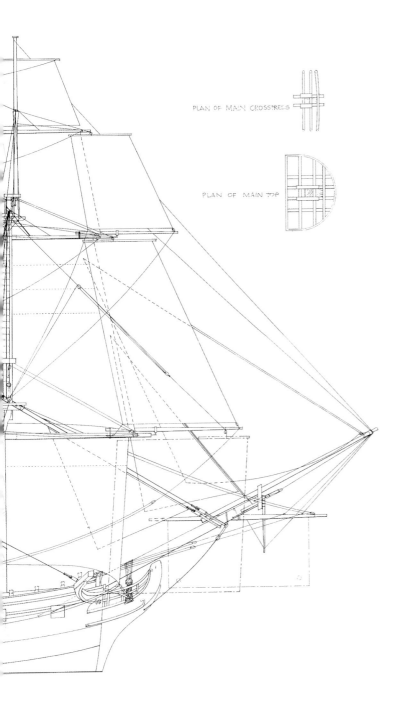

PLAN OF MAIN CROSSTREES

PLAN OF MAIN TOP

The main source for the 4-metre frigates was David MacGregor's *Three Sisters* taken from David Steel's *Shipbuilders Vade Mecum* (1805), the plan of which is shown here. The dimensions for the masts and spars were taken from the tables in the book *Eighteenth-Century Rigs and Rigging* by Marquardt. Many of the other details were taken from books and contemporary paintings. Scale as shown.

(Source: author)

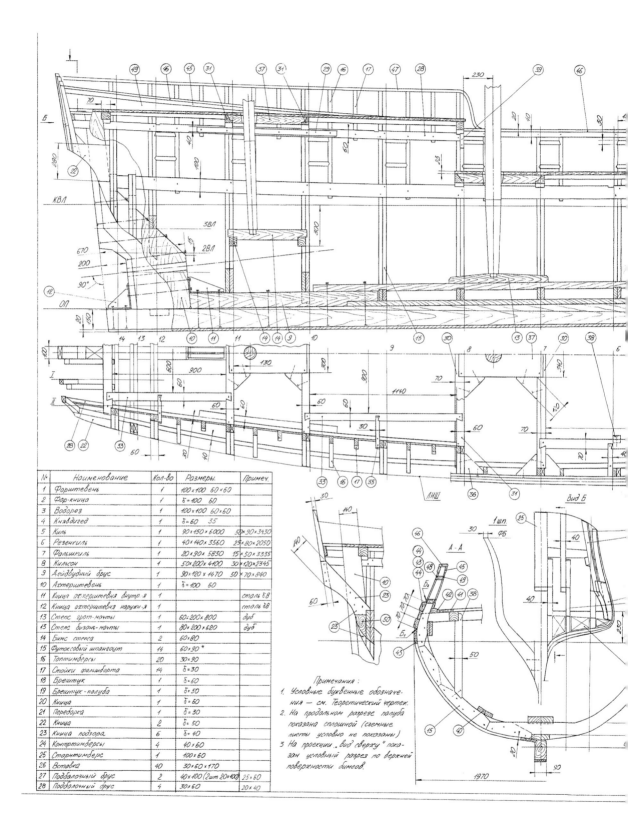

№	Наименование	Кол-во	Размеры	Примеч.
1	Форштевень	1	100×100	50×50
2	Фор-кница	1	δ=100	50
3	Водорез	1	100×100	50×50
4	Княвдигед	1	δ=50	35
5	Киль	1	90×150×6000	50×90×3430
6	Резенкиль	1	40×40×3560	25×80×2050
7	Фальшкиль	1	20×90×5830	15×50×3335
8	Кильсон	1	50×200×4400	30×120×2345
9	Дейдвудный брус	1	90×120×1470	50×70×840
10	Ахтерштевень	1	δ=100	50
11	Кница ахтерштевня внутр-я	1		сталь δ8
12	Кница ахтерштевня наружн-я	1		сталь δ8
13	Степс грот-мачты	1	60×200×800	дуб
13	Степс бизань-мачты	1	80×200×620	дуб
14	Бимс степса	2	60×80	
15	Футоксовый шпангоут	14	60×90 *	
16	Топтимберсы	20	30×90	
17	Стойки фальшборта	14	δ=30	
18	Брештук	1	δ=60	
19	Брештук-полуба	1	δ=50	
20	Кница	1	δ=60	
21	Переборка	1	δ=30	
22	Кница	2	δ=50	
23	Кница подзора	6	δ=40	
24	Контртимберсы	4	40×60	
25	Стартимберс	1	100×60	
26	Вставка	40	30×60×170	
27	Поддалочный брус	2	40×100 (2шт 20×100)	25×60
28	Поддалочный брус	4	30×60	20×40

Примечания:
1. Условные буквенные обозначения — см. Теоретический чертеж.
2. На продольном разрезе палуба показана сплошной (съемные листы условно не показаны)
3. На проекции „вид сверху" показан условный разрез по верхней поверхности бимсов.

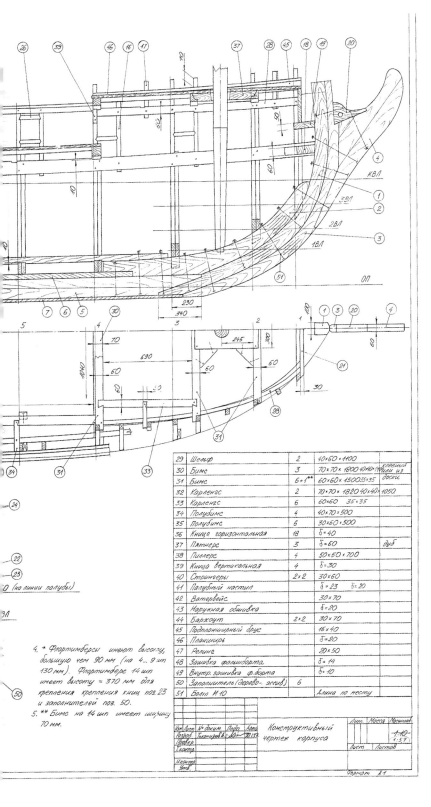

This is a construction drawing drafted by Pavel Martuikov for the construction of the 4-metre frigates. It shows the proposed construction method for the frames of the models, which is a similar method to full-sized practice. The method eventually used was much simplified and saved time. It is worth noting that this drawing shows the model to be fitted with a propeller to drive it through the water. Engines were never fitted to any of the models, although it had been proposed early on. No scale.

(Source: author)

29	Шельф	2	40×60×1100	
30	Бимс	3	70×70×1800 40×40×1	клеенный или из досок
31	Бимс	5+1**	60×60×1500 35×35	
32	Карленгс	2	70×70×1820 40×40×1050	
33	Карленгс	6	60×60 35×35	
34	Полубимс	4	40×70×500	
35	Полубимс	6	30×60×500	
36	Кница горизонтальная	18	δ=40	
37	Пяртнерс	3	δ=60	дуб
38	Пиллерс	4	50×50×700	
39	Кница вертикальная	4	δ=30	
40	Стрингеры	2×2	30×60	
41	Палубный настил		δ=23 δ=20	
42	Ватервейс		30×70	
43	Наружная обшивка		δ=20	
44	Бархоут	2×2	30×70	
45	Подпланширный брус		15×40	
46	Планширь		δ=20	
47	Реlinг		20×50	
48	Зашивка фальшборта		δ=14	
49	Внутр. зашивка ф.борта		δ=10	
50	Заполнитель (дерево-эпсив)	6		
51	Болт М10		Длина по месту	

4. * Флортимберсы имеют высоту, большую чем 90 мм (на 4...9 шп 130 мм). Флортимберс 14 шп имеет высоту ≈ 370 мм для крепления крепления книц поз.23 и заполнителей поз. 50.

5. ** Бимс на 14 шп имеет ширину 70 мм.

Конструктивный чертеж корпуса

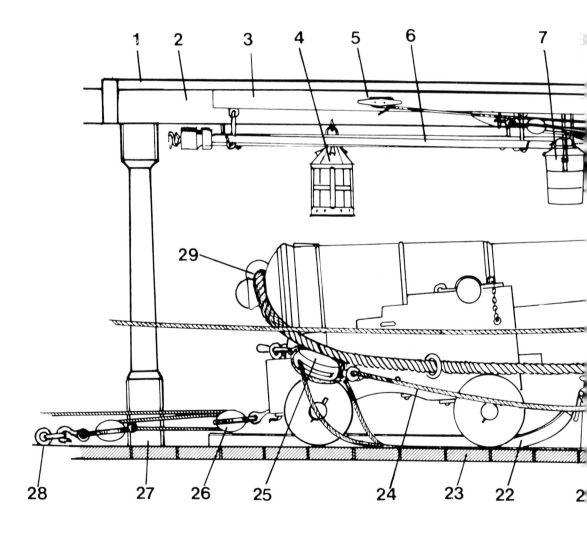

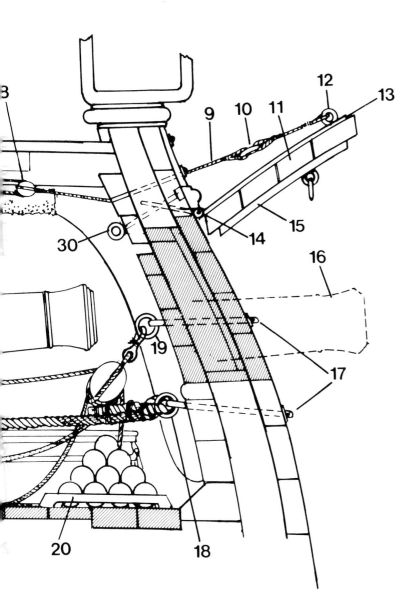

The port side profile of a 12pdr cannon on the frigate *Essex*'s gundeck. Such interior detail was not needed for the models that we built; instead, dummy barrels were constructed and placed. No scale.

1. Gangboard
2. Skid beam
3. Ledge
4. Lantern
5. Port tackle cleat
6. Gun tackle implements
7. Fire bucket
8. Gun port tackle
9. Port lanyard
10. Lanyard ring
11. Gun port lid
12. Eyebolt
13. Gun port lid strap
14. Port hinge
15. Port lid lining
16. 12pdr (run out)
17. Through hull bolts
18. Breeching bolt
19. Gun tackle ringbolt
20. Shot rack
21. Sponge tub
22. Crooked hand spike
23. Gun deck
24. 12pdr gun carriage
25. Gun tackle
26. Train tackle
27. Pillar
28. Ringbolt
29. Breeching rope
30. Securing eyebolt
(Source: Takajian, 1990)

of slightly different design they were dimensionally the same. Although the sails were interchangeable, they were made to follow the historical practice of the nationalities they portrayed. For example we found, after research, that there was a hole in the lower corners of the spritsail which was a different size for each nation and these were included.

Profile of a 32-gun frigate: *Essex*

32-gun and smaller, 24-gun ships served with all the major navies of the Napoleonic era. *Essex* was an American ship, although some of its component parts were imported from England.

Date entered into service	1799
Rating	Fifth
Length of gun deck	141ft
Depth of hold	12ft 3in
Breadth of beam	37ft
Tonnage	850 tons
Number of guns	1799: ten 6pdrs; twenty-six 12pdrs. 1811: forty 32pdr carronades; six 12pdrs
Crew complement	319
Cost of building (excluding government supplies)	$75,473

(Source: Takakjian 1990)

The Baltic Trader Julia

The full-sized *Julia* is a wooden Baltic trader built in the 1930s and was the second choice ship for the Hornblower team. The first vessel that was found by the production company had three masts and it was on this ship that the replica models were originally based. Construction of the two models had reached a stage where the hulls were virtually complete when the message arrived to stop work, since the company had decided against buying the first choice ship because it was 'hogged' (meaning that its back was broken). There then ensued a mad scramble as a world-wide search was commenced to find and secure a replacement at short notice. Meanwhile, the two models were causing me a great deal of concern because they were needed very early on in the shooting schedule and we could not complete their construction within the tight constraints of the schedule. When the replacement – *Julia* – was eventually found she was somewhere in the Baltic and we needed her in the Black Sea. Moreover, she required a considerable programme of

The model of the *Julia* at her moorings in the tank at Pinewood.

A close up of *Julia* being prepared for filming. A good deal of her deck detailing can be seen in this picture. All of the fittings and hatchways in the bow area were removable, to allow access to the hatches which were covering the access into the hull.

conversion work before filming could start. To add to the problems which we faced, there were no drawings for us to base the models on and they were eventually constructed using photographs of the full-sized ship taken from various angles. The models followed the same construction method as the others, being cold moulded below the waterline with strip planking above.

The *Julia* was built nearly two centuries later than the Hornblower period and therefore had many modern features in her rigging and deck layout. The rig had much more metal than a ship of Nelson's era and used steel wire and chain in its rigging. The shrouds on the full-sized ship are set up with steel wire coming down to large bottle screws which anchor them in place. Topsy, the skipper of *Julia*, hid these modern devices behind mock ups of deadeyes and lanyards and very effective they were too. On the models the shrouds were set up on deadeyes in time-honoured fashion. An extra yard arm was installed on the fore mast of *Julia* to try to give her a more square-rigged look, but it was very difficult to convince anybody that she was not fore-and-aft rigged. There was talk about fitting gun ports on the *Julia*, but in the end, due to the lack of suitable space and time, she eventually was seen with a few swivel guns around her stern only when occasion required. The full-sized *Julia* is fitted with a large diesel engine as an auxiliary

means of propulsion; no effort was made to give any suggestion of this in the model. The exhaust pipe for the diesel came up through the deck and because it was so noticeable it was disguised with a barrel mounted on the deck. The models also replicated this feature. Her modern anchor winches in the bow were hidden behind dummy cabins and lockers.

Julia played many different roles in the production including the *Caroline*, *Claudette*, *Le Pique*, *Marie Galante*, and she was also used in a number of harbour scenes. One of the *Julia* models was sunk eight times in an afternoon for the scene with the expanding rice. To play all of these different roles, small yet conspicuous visible features on the decks were changed. For example, a scroll was added foreword of the aft rail. At various times she was black all over, had a broad ochre band along her sides and at other times her decoration was picked out in white. The stern was shown with and without decoration and sometimes a boat hung from her stern davits, whilst on other occasions the davits were completely removed. *Julia*'s modern anchors were dressed up with enlarged stocks (the wooden cross piece at the top), to give her the appearance of a ship from a much earlier era.

Julia is a wooden Baltic trader built in the 1930s. Many such small wooden sailing craft were built around the shores of the Baltic by farming communities. Life was hard in these northern waters and many villages would build small trading craft to transport tar (taken from trees), fish and timber. The crews would work part time on their farms and the rest of the time would be spent with the ships.

The Fireships

The concept of a fireship is a very old one with their most notable success being their employment by Drake against the Spanish Armada. Fireships were not used in the wars against France, although the Royal Navy did keep a number available throughout this period; thirteen were on the Navy List in 1799. They were usually converted merchant ships of around 300 to 400 tons and were 'fitted as sloops'. In 1808 the last fireships on the Navy List were reclassed as ship sloops, effectively ending their use.

The most notable external feature of a fireship was that the gunports were hinged at the bottom so the ports would open downwards, allowing air in to feed the fire. Internally they had a 'fire room' which was filled with combustible materials and had brass or copper chimneys fitted into the deck to direct the fire into the rigging. The ships' guns would also be loaded, so that when the flames reached them they would discharge themselves, adding to the melee.

Fireships were required for the Hornblower series, as Hornblower's examination to become a Lieutenant is interrupted by a Spanish fireship sailing into Gibraltar. Three fireship models were built for the production, with the idea that at least one would be totally destroyed during filming; this would leave two in reserve for unforeseen eventualities and mishaps during the filming process. When the fireship sequence was eventually filmed at Pinewood, only one of the models was used and the damage from the fire was minimal, mostly effecting the rigging and spars and leaving the hull virtually intact.

Of the two remaining models one was never used and the other was remodelled to be the third replica of HMS *Indefatigable*. This work was started by a modelmaker in the Yalta studios, brought in as an outside contractor. He had a very difficult task, as only minimal tools, materials and resources were available. The problem of converting the fireship model into HMS *Indefatigable* was compounded by the fact that the hulls were of a different shape and design. Additionally, HMS *Indefatigable* had three masts, whereas the fireship had two – which were of entirely different structure and proportions. The conversion work was completed by the craftsman at Pinewood using spars and sails from other models.

Of all the models, the fireships were the simplest to build and were completed first. They gave the modelmakers some very good practice for the more complex models that were built later. They had virtually no deck detail except on the poop deck, where there was a wheel and binnacle and a very simplified sail plan and rigging.

Much of the 'live' action in the fireship sequence takes place on the poop deck of the ship with Hornblower and Foster struggling to save HMS *Indefatigable* from the burning fireship. It was all filmed on a purpose-built set at Artek near Yalta. The set was a full-sized mock-up of the after part of the ship, built on land over-

A model of HMS *Indefatigable* after a battle with the French. This model was converted from one of the fireships.

looking the sea. At one point during the action Foster falls through the burning deck and has to be rescued by Hornblower. This area of the deck had been specially constructed using balsa wood, to ensure it was not strong enough to support a man's weight. This special effect was constructed and tested by Derek Langley and Graham Aikman. Derek had an unfortunate accident with this weakened deck when he inadvertently stepped on it and went through it without any of the crash mattresses below to break his fall. He damaged his arm and it was subsequently put into a sling for a time although he thankfully made a full recovery.

Profile of a fireship: *Rocket*

Fireships were intentionally set on fire and launched against enemy ships in an attempt to burn them or create disorder. Fireships emerged in the Royal Navy in the 1630s, and were occasionally used until 1808.

Date entered into service	1804
Rating	Paid as a Fifth rate ship
Length of gun deck	52ft 41/2in
Depth of hold	17ft
Tonnage	62 tons
Number of guns	4 guns
Crew complement	8 men
Cost of building	£350

(Source: Coggeshall 1997)

Models built for the series

Names as seen in films	Type	Based on	Hull length	Number built	Comments
Justinian	74-gun ship	*Le Superbe* (French 3rd rate)	5 metres	1	Also played a Spanish warship
Indefatigable, Papillon	20-gun ship	*Grand Turk* & *Blandford*	7 metres and 5.5 metres	2	7 metre model not used – a fireship was converted instead
No names	Frigate	Chapman's drawings, *Pandora* & many other sources	4 meters	3	These models played many roles in the whole series
Claudette, Le Reve, Caroline, Maire Gallante, Le Pique, Spanish Merchant Ship	Baltic trader	*Julia*	4.5 metres	2	1 model modified for sinking
No names	Fireships	*Fair American*	4.5 metres	3	1 used (burnt), 1 converted into a third *Indefatigable*

Bibliography & References

Many people, too numerous to mention individually by name, were sources of information and help for the production of the Hornblower models. I have listed the sources that I used for the building of the models and for the writing of this book below. This is by no means a definitive list used for the whole production, because other departments – for example costume – would have had their own sources.

Archibald E. H. H. *The Wooden Fighting Ship in the Navy AD 896-1890*, 1972.

Boudriot, Jean. *The Seventy-Four Gun Ship*, Vols 1,2,3 and 4, 1986.

Chapelle, Howard I. *The History of American Sailing Ships*, 1982.

Chapman, Frederik. *Architectura Navalis Mercatoria*, 1971.

Coggeshall, James L. 'The fireship and its role in the Royal Navy', unpublished MA thesis, Texas A&M University, 1997.

Forester, C. S. *The Young Hornblower Omnibus*, 1989.

Gardiner, Robert. *The First Frigates, Nine-pounder and Twelve-pounder Frigates, 1748-1815*, 1992.

Gardiner, Robert. *The Heavy Frigate, Eighteen Pounder Frigates*, Vol 1, 1994.

Gardiner, Robert. (ed.) *The Line of Battle, The Sailing Warship 1650-1840*, (The History of the Ship series) 1994.

Gardiner, Robert. (ed.) *The Heyday of Sail, The Merchant Sailing Ship 1650-1830*, 1995.

Goodwin, Peter. *The Construction and Fitting of the Sailing Man of War 1650-1850*, 1987.

Goodwin, Peter. *The 20-gun Ship Blandford*, 1988.

Habron, John D. *Trafalgar and the Spanish Navy*, 1988.

Harland, John. *Seamanship in the Age of Sail*, 1996.

Kemp, Peter. (ed.) *The Oxford Companion to Ships and the Sea*, 1976.

Kemp, Peter and Ormond, Richard. *The Great Age of Sail*, 1986.

Lavery, Brian. *The Ship of the Line*, Vol 1 (1983) and 2 (1984).

Lavery, Brian. *The 74-gun Ship Bellona*, 1985.

Lavery, Brian. *The Arming and Fitting of Ships of War*, 1600-1815, 1987.

Lavery, Brian. *Building the Wooden Walls, the Design and Construction of the 74-gun Ship Valiant,* 1991.

Lavery, Brian. *Nelson's Navy, The Ships, Men and Organisation*, 1783-1815, 1994.

Lees, James. *The Masting and Rigging of English Ships of War 1625-1860*, 1990.

Longridge, C. Nepean. *The Anatomy of Nelson's Ships*, 1955.

Lyon, David. *The Age of Nelson, Sea battles in Close-up*, 1996.

Lyon, David. *The Sailing Navy List, All the ships of the Royal Navy, Built, Purchased and Captured, 1688-1860*, 1997.

MacGregor, David. *Merchant Sailing Ships, Sovereignty of Sail, 1775-1815*, 1985.

Marquardt, Karl Heinz. *Eighteenth-century Rigs and Rigging*, 1986.

McKay, John. *The 100-gun Ship Victory*, 1987.

McKay, John and Coleman, Ron. *The 24-gun Frigate Pandora 1779*, 1992.

Takakjian, Portia. *The 32-gun Frigate Essex*, 1990.

Warner, Oliver. *Great Sea Battles*, 1968.

White, David. *The Frigate Diana*, 1987.

Wilson, Timothy. *Flags at Sea*, 1986.

Index

Picture & quotation credits

The photographs reproduced within this book are © Martin Saville with the exception of:
page 66-67: Painting by Nicholas Pocock. Courtesy of National Maritime Museum, London
page 68-69: Painting by Ross Watton. First published in Conway Maritime Press' *The 74-gun Ship Bellona.*

The draughts reproduced within this book are © Martin Saville unless noted below:
page 90-91: First published in Conway Maritime Press' *The 74-gun Ship Bellona.*
        © Brian Lavery 1985
page 92-93: First published in Conway Maritime Press' *The 74-gun Ship Bellona.*
        © Brian Lavery 1985
page 104-105: First published in Conway Maritime Press' *The 20-gun Ship Blandford.*
        © Peter Goodwin 1988
page 106-107: First published in Conway Maritime Press' *The 20-gun Ship Blandford.*
        © Peter Goodwin 1988
page 110-111: First published in Conway Maritime Press' *The 32-gun Frigate Essex.*
        © Portia Takajian 1990
page 112-113: Drawn by David MacGregor.
page 116-117: First published in Conway Maritime Press' *The 32-gun Frigate Essex.*
        © Portia Takajian 1990

The quotations reproduced within this book are from the following sources:
page 8: C. S. Forester, *Mr. Midshipman Hornblower*, in *The Young Hornblower*, page 10.
page 21: C. S. Forester, *Mr. Midshipman Hornblower*, in *The Young Hornblower*, page 155.
page 53: C. S. Forester, *Lieutenant Hornblower*, in *The Young Hornblower*, page 285.
page 81: C. S. Forester, *Mr. Midshipman Hornblower*, in *The Young Hornblower*, page 163.
page 85: C. S. Forester, *Hornblower and the 'Hotspur'*, in *The Young Hornblower*, page 449.
From *The Young Hornblower*, Omnibus edition, C. S. Forester. London 1964, 1989.